THE ROMAN EMPIRE – A CONCISE GUIDE

From Caesars to soldiers, gladiators to gods — the story that made Rome the empire of empires, and that still shapes our world

James Burrows

© **Copyright 2025 - All rights reserved.**

The content contained within this book may not be reproduced, duplicated or transmitted without direct written permission from the author or the publisher.

Under no circumstances will any blame or legal responsibility be held against the publisher, or author, for any damages, reparation, or monetary loss due to the information contained within this book, either directly or indirectly.

<u>Legal Notice:</u>

This book is copyright protected. It is only for personal use. You cannot amend, distribute, sell, use, quote or paraphrase any part, or the content within this book, without the consent of the author or publisher.

<u>Disclaimer Notice:</u>

Please note the information contained within this document is for educational and entertainment purposes only. All effort has been executed to present accurate, up to date, reliable, complete information. No warranties of any kind are declared or implied. Readers acknowledge that the author is not engaged in the rendering of legal, financial, medical or professional advice. The content within this book has been derived from various sources. Please consult a licensed professional before attempting any techniques outlined in this book.

By reading this document, the reader agrees that under no circumstances is the author responsible for any losses, direct or indirect, that are incurred as a result of the use of the information contained within this document, including, but not limited to, errors, omissions, or inaccuracies.

Other Books by James Burrows

What You Need To Know:

World War I for Teens
World War I for Kids
World War II for Teens
World War II for Kids
World War II for Teens – 21 Special Operations
World War II for Teens – The Secret War
World War II for Teens – The Holocaust
World War II – The Pacific War
The Vietnam War for Teens

The Ultimate Guide:

Egyptian Mythology for Kids
Greek Mythology for Kids
Norse Mythology for Kids

Concise Guides:

A History of Israel and Palestine
Alexander the Great - One Man. One Empire. One Legacy.

Other Books:

The Art of War – Sun Tzu
Meditations – Marcus Aurelius

CONTENTS

INTRODUCTION : THE WORLD ROME MADE

PART I: FOUNDATIONS OF EMPIRE

Chapter 1: Before the Empire – The Roman Kingdom and Republic

Chapter 2: The Birth of the Empire

PART II: ROME AT ITS HEIGHT

Chapter 3: Emperors and Power – Who Ruled Rome

Chapter 4: A World Empire – Size, Provinces, and Borders

Chapter 5: Legions and Conquest – How Rome Won an Empire

Chapter 6. The Cities of the Roman Empire – Jewels of Stone and Marble

Chapter 7: Great Romans – Masters of War, Thought, and Statecraft and Their Enemies

Chapter 8. Roman Science, Technology, and the Economy

PART III: DAILY LIFE IN THE ROMAN EMPIRE

Chapter 9: Life in the City and Countryside

Chapter 10: Family, Religion, and Society

Chapter 11: Blood and Sand – The World of Gladiators

Chapter 12: Slavery and Class in the Roman World

PART IV: DECLINE AND LEGACY

Chapter 13: Crisis and Fall of the Western Empire

Chapter 14: The Eastern Empire and Byzantium

Chapter 15: The Enduring Legacy of Rome

EPILOGUE

APPENDICES

- Timeline of Key Events (753 BC – 1453 AD)
- Glossary of Roman Terms and Titles
- List of Emperors

ABOUT THE AUTHOR

INTRODUCTION – THE WORLD ROME MADE

Julius Caesar stood on the Capitoline Hill, the city spread before him in the golden haze of late afternoon. From here, Rome was a living mosaic - the marble gleam of temples, the hum of markets in the Forum, the tramp of legionaries on the cobbled streets, and beyond, the crowded insulae (apartment buildings) where tens of thousands lived stacked upon one another in brick and timber. It was a city of senators and slaves, of triumphal arches and beggars' bowls, of soaring ambition and relentless hunger.

Capitoline Hill, Rome

Caesar had seen its reach stretch far beyond these walls. He had crossed the Rhine and stared into the forests of Germany, landed on the mist-wreathed shores of Britain, and subdued the proud tribes of Gaul. He knew that Rome's destiny no longer lay within Italy alone, but in the vast dominions wrested from rivals, built with the blood and discipline of her legions. Rome was no longer a republic of farmers, it was an empire in all but name.

And yet, as he looked upon the city he had reshaped with victories and reforms, Caesar knew that glory came at a price. Rome was rich, powerful, and restless. Senators plotted, friends turned rivals, and the people adored their champions only to cast them down in the next breath. He himself would soon feel that truth carved in knives beneath the portico of Pompey's Theatre.

But Caesar's vision, of a Rome unchallenged, ordered, and eternal, would not die with him. His heir, Octavian, would take up the mantle, calling himself Augustus, and with him the age of emperors would begin. Rome would stand as the mistress of the known world, her legions marching from the Atlantic to the Euphrates, her laws shaping provinces, her culture binding a patchwork of peoples into a single world.

For centuries Rome endured, her triumphs and tragedies written not only in stone, but in the memories of all who lived under her rule. And though her empire eventually crumbled in the West, her spirit remained, in the arches and aqueducts, in the languages and laws, in the very idea of civilization itself.

This is the story of that Rome - of conquest and collapse, of emperors and citizens, of an empire that rose from a small city on the Tiber to shape the course of human history.

WHY ROME STILL MATTERS

Two millennia ago, a civilization thrived whose capital housed over a million people. It boasted tourism and luxury resorts, high-rise apartment blocks, fast-food outlets, efficient urban administration, water supply, transport systems, and mass entertainment, achievements unmatched until the modern era.

The Roman Empire spanned centuries and there is no escaping its shadow. Across Europe, North Africa, and the Middle East, its echoes still ring, in ruined forums and crumbling roads, in the Latin roots of our languages, in our legal systems and political ideas. Even our calendar is based on the Julian calendar, introduced by Julius Caesar. Rome may have fallen more than 1,500 years ago but it gave us the structure on which much of modern civilization rests.

This book is a concise journey through that legacy. It does not aim to capture every emperor, battle, or decree, but instead, it covers Rome's extraordinary story from the myths of Romulus and Remus to the thunder of the Colosseum; from

Caesar's campaigns in Gaul to the sack of Rome; from the lives of senators and slaves to the resilience of the Byzantine East, this is the tale of how a small Italian city-state rose to command the known world.

We will bring Rome to life in all its complexity: brutal and brilliant, ordered and chaotic, ruthless yet astonishingly creative. Along the way, look out for some amazing facts and curiosities that show how strange and extraordinary Roman life could be, such as:

❖ DID YOU KNOW

- *In the 2nd century AD, the Roman Empire had an estimated population of around 65 million people, probably around a quarter of the world's population at the time.*

- *Roman concrete, mixing volcanic ash with quicklime, was self-healing. The Pantheon in Rome, built in 125 AD, is still the world's largest unsupported concrete dome.*

- *The streets of ancient Rome were covered in graffiti, much like modern cities. Graffiti was a commonly used and popular political tool. If the Roman people were unhappy with something they would paint it on walls of buildings.*

To study Rome is to hold up a mirror to ourselves, to see how ideas of power, citizenship, law, and culture have evolved, and to recognize that the echoes of Roman triumphs and failures still speak to us across the gulf of time.

This is not just the story of a fallen empire. It is the story of the enduring idea of Rome, of an empire that, though gone, remains eternal.

PART I: FOUNDATIONS OF EMPIRE

CHAPTER 1: BEFORE THE EMPIRE – THE ROMAN KINGDOM AND REPUBLIC

Origins of Rome: Myth and Archaeology (753 BC)

The story of Rome begins in myth, with the famous tale of Romulus and Remus, twin brothers born to the vestal virgin Rhea Silvia and the god Mars, the Roman god of war. Abandoned and left to die by their grandfather, the King Amulius, the twins were discovered by a she-wolf who nursed them. They were later found by a shepherd, Faustulus, who raised them alongside his wife, Acca Larentia. As they grew, Romulus and Remus eventually led a rebellion against Amulius, restoring their grandfather's throne.

Their story culminated in a dispute over where to found a city. The brothers chose different sites, and Romulus, the more determined of the two, ultimately killed Remus in a fit of anger after Remus mocked his city's walls. Romulus then named the city after himself: Rome. This dramatic origin myth encapsulated the Romans' belief in the city's divine favor and predestined greatness, a city born from conflict and destined for power.

Beneath this myth, archaeology provides a more tangible foundation for Rome's beginnings. Situated on the Tiber River, Rome was one of many early settlements in the Italian peninsula. Archaeological evidence points to the establishment of Rome around 753 BC, where early villages began to emerge on the seven hills surrounding the river. These settlements grew through a combination of indigenous Latin and Sabine people, combined with the influence of neighboring Etruscans and other Italic tribes.

The Roman Kingdom (753–509 BC)

With Romulus as its first king, the Roman Kingdom period of 753–509 BC began. Though much of the early history of the kingdom is steeped in legend, there are historical aspects to consider. During this time, Rome was ruled by kings, who wielded both military and political power.

The kingdom was not a hereditary monarchy in the modern sense, as kingship was largely determined by the Senate, an advisory council of aristocrats. Over time, the kings would grow in influence, and some, like Tarquinius Priscus, took power by force. Rome's kings, some of whom may have been of Etruscan origin, played a critical role in laying the foundation for Roman civilization. They were instrumental in urban development, establishing the first temples, forums, and roads, which would define Roman life for centuries.

The Etruscans, whose civilization dominated the central Italian peninsula, were particularly influential in the development of early Rome. Their architecture, religion, and even political organization had a profound impact on the Romans. Etruscan kings are credited with building Rome's first major city walls, the construction of temples to the gods, and the establishment of key religious rituals. These influences were not only architectural but also cultural, as Rome absorbed aspects of Etruscan technology, language, and organization.

❖ DID YOU KNOW

- *The Etruscans were a sophisticated ancient people of central Italy, flourishing before Rome, whose origins remain debated but are thought to be either native to Italy or from the eastern Mediterranean.*

Rome's society, during the Roman Kingdom, was highly structured. The king was at the top of the social pyramid, with an elite group of noble families forming the ruling class. Beneath them were the common citizens and the slaves, who made up a large portion of the population. Despite this stratification, the monarchy itself was vulnerable to change, as power was not centralized in one family. This instability eventually led to the overthrow of the monarchy.

The fall of the last king, Tarquinius Superbus (Tarquin the Proud), in 509 BC marked the end of the Roman Kingdom and the establishment of the Roman Republic. According to the tradition, the tyrannical reign of Tarquin, particularly his son's rape of a noblewoman named Lucretia, ignited a rebellion, and the Romans vowed never to live under a king again. The overthrow of Tarquin marked the dawn of a new era, one where the people would govern themselves, at least in theory.

The Roman Republic (509–27 BC)

The shift from monarchy to republic marked a revolutionary change in Rome's political and social structures. The Roman Republic (509–27 BC) was defined by the rule of law and a system of checks and balances, where power was divided among elected officials and a Senate. The Republic was based on a belief in the sovereignty of the people, though the reality was a system dominated by a small elite of patrician families.

❖ DID YOU KNOW

- *Rome was the first city in the world to record a population of 1 million, taken from the first census in the 2nd Century BC. The next city in Europe to have a population of this size was Victorian London in the 19th Century!*

The Senate, Consuls, and Republican Government

At the core of the Roman Republic was its Senate, a body of aristocrats who held great influence over policy and military matters. The Senate's members were not elected, but appointed, typically from the most powerful and wealthy families in Rome. Over time, the Senate would become the heart of Roman government, advising magistrates and playing a key role in foreign and domestic policy.

The consuls were the chief magistrates of the Republic, elected annually by the people. Each year, two consuls were chosen to serve as joint heads of government. They had executive powers, commanded the army, and presided over the Senate and assemblies. This system ensured that power was not concentrated in the hands of a single individual, but it also created potential for conflict and political rivalry.

The Roman assemblies allowed for a limited form of democratic participation. These were bodies of Roman citizens who could vote on laws and elect magistrates. However, the right to vote was restricted to adult male citizens, and the wealthy were able to exercise far more influence than the poorer citizens.

The Conflict of the Orders – Patricians vs Plebeians

The early years of the Republic were marked by a struggle between two social classes: the patricians and the plebeians. The patricians were the old aristocratic families who held most of the political power and land. The plebeians, on the other hand, were the common people such as farmers, merchants, and artisans. They had little political power and were often at the mercy of the patricians.

The Conflict of the Orders refers to the series of struggles between these two groups over political and social equality. The plebeians, feeling oppressed by the aristocratic elite, fought for greater rights and representation. One of the major turning points in this conflict was the establishment of the tribunes of the plebs in 494 BC, officials who were elected to protect plebeian interests. Over time, the plebeians gained more influence, securing access to key offices and eventually winning the right to pass laws.

Expansion Through Italy and Mediterranean Conquests

As Rome consolidated its internal structure, it began to look outward, first conquering the surrounding cities and peoples of the Italian peninsula. Through a combination of military conquest, alliances, and diplomacy, Rome gradually expanded its territory over the course of several centuries.

The early campaigns in Italy were punctuated by the Samnite Wars (343–290 BC), in which Rome defeated a coalition of mountain tribes in central Italy. With these victories, Rome solidified its control over much of Italy and set its sights on expanding beyond its borders.

Rome's Punic Wars with the powerful city-state of Carthage (located near modern day Tunis in Tunisia) (264–146 BC) were a defining series of conflicts. The

First Punic War resulted in Rome's control of Sicily, the first Roman province. The Second Punic War saw the famous Carthaginian general Hannibal invade Italy and defeat Roman forces at the Battle of Cannae, but Rome eventually triumphed. The Third Punic War saw the total destruction of Carthage, solidifying Rome as the dominant power in the Mediterranean.

Civil Wars, Julius Caesar's Rise, and the End of the Republic

By the 1st century BC, Rome's political system had become increasingly unstable. Power struggles between rival generals and politicians culminated in a series of civil wars. The rise of powerful figures like Julius Caesar signaled the end of the Republic.

Caesar, a brilliant general and politician, conquered Gaul (modern France) and gained the loyalty of his army. When the Senate ordered him to disband his army and return to Rome, Caesar famously crossed the Rubicon River in 49 BC, declaring civil war. After a series of bloody battles, Caesar emerged victorious and declared himself dictator for life.

Julius Caesar

Despite his popularity with the people, Caesar's rise to power alarmed the Senate. Fearing that he would establish a monarchy, a group of senators conspired to assassinate him on the Ides of March (March 15) in 44 BC. His death led to another round of civil wars, culminating in the rise of Octavian (later Augustus), Caesar's adopted son, who would bring an end to the Republic and lay the foundations for the Roman Empire.

❖ DID YOU KNOW

- *Julius Caesar hated going bald so he made it illegal for anyone to stand above him and look down at his bald patch - if you did, you could be put to death!*

- *Julius Caesar led 2 invasions of Britain, in 55 and 54 BC, extending Roman influence beyond the Republic's usual frontiers. Though they achieved no lasting conquest, the campaigns demonstrated his ambition, resolve, and skill in logistics.*

- *Caesar was kidnapped by pirates around 78 BC while crossing the Aegean Sea. He told his captors the ransom they had demanded was not high enough and promised to crucify them when he was free, which they thought a joke. On his release he raised a fleet, captured them and did have them crucified, mercifully ordering their throats cut first.*

Caesar and Cleopatra

In 48 BC, Caesar arrived in Alexandria during his pursuit of Pompey. Cleopatra, then about 21, famously had herself smuggled into his quarters (legend says rolled in a carpet or a linen sack). Caesar supported Cleopatra in her dynastic struggle against her brother Ptolemy XIII. After Ptolemy's death, Cleopatra was confirmed as Queen of Egypt with Caesar's backing.

Their relationship lasted throughout Caesar's time in Egypt. When Cleopatra later visited Rome (46–44 BC), she stayed in one of Caesar's villas across the Tiber.

Julius Caesar and Cleopatra had a son in 47 BC: Ptolemy XV Philopator Philometor Caesar, better known as Caesarion ("little Caesar"). Caesar never officially acknowledged Caesarion as his heir (his will named Octavian - later Augustus - as his successor). Romans were skeptical, and some dismissed Caesarion's paternity.

As we will see in the next chapter, after Caesar's assassination in 44 BC, Cleopatra returned to Egypt with Caesarion, making him her co-ruler. When Cleopatra and Mark Antony were defeated by Octavian (31–30 BC), Octavian captured Alexandria.

In 30 BC, after Cleopatra's suicide, Caesarion was executed on Octavian's orders, reportedly persuaded by the maxim "Too many Caesars is not a good thing." He was about 17 years old.

Caesarion was the last Pharaoh of Egypt of the Ptolemaic line. With his death, Egypt became a Roman province under Octavian.

❖ DID YOU KNOW

- *"Caesar" shifted from being a personal name to an imperial title. Emperors first used it to stress their link to Julius Caesar and legitimize their rule, and over time it became a standard part of the imperial title, though not every ruler adopted it.*

CHAPTER 2: THE BIRTH OF THE EMPIRE

Caesar's Assassination (44 BC) and the Rise of Octavian

The assassination of Julius Caesar in 44 BC (at 55 years old) marked the brutal end of the Roman Republic. Caesar had spent the last decade of his life consolidating power, and his appointment as dictator for life was seen by many as the final step in the fall of the Republic. His rule had fundamentally altered the balance of power, with the Senate growing increasingly disillusioned by his authoritarianism. Yet, despite his sweeping reforms and military successes, Caesar's reign alienated many of the traditional ruling class, setting the stage for a fateful conspiracy.

On the Ides of March, a group of senators led by Brutus and Cassius assassinated Caesar in the Senate House. The death of Rome's most powerful figure sent shockwaves throughout the empire. Far from restoring the Republic, it plunged Rome into chaos. Caesar's supporters and rivals alike sought to fill the power vacuum, but the civil wars that ensued would not end until the final triumph of one man: Octavian, Caesar's grandnephew and adopted son.

The assassination of Julius Caesar

In the wake of Caesar's death, Octavian, then just 18 years old, began his ascent. Despite being initially underestimated, he was the rightful heir to Caesar's legacy, both politically and militarily. With the support of Caesar's veterans, Octavian formed an alliance with Mark Antony, Caesar's closest lieutenant, and Lepidus to form the Second Triumvirate, a political coalition aimed at avenging Caesar's death and defeating his enemies.

The Triumvirs hunted down Caesar's assassins and secured their rule. However, tensions soon emerged between the two more powerful members of the Triumvirate, Octavian and Antony. As the alliance unraveled, Octavian's ambitions clashed with Antony's growing ties to Cleopatra VII, Queen of Egypt. The seeds of rivalry were sown, and it was only a matter of time before one of them would emerge victorious.

▫▫DID YOU KNOW

- *A famous line is linked to Caesar's assassination - "Et tu, Brute?" ("And you, Brutus?"), said to be Caesar's words upon seeing Brutus, once his trusted ally, among the assassins*

- *Caesar's wife, Calpurnia, begged him not to attend his meetings on March 15, after waking from a nightmare in which she held her husband's corpse. Caesar initially agreed, but after mocking from senators, he changed his mind, with fateful consequences!*

The Battle of Actium and the Defeat of Mark Antony and Cleopatra

The defining moment in the struggle between Octavian and Antony came at the Battle of Actium in 31 BC. The battle was fought off the coast of Greece, near the city of Actium, and was the culmination of a series of military and diplomatic struggles between the two men. Antony, who had allied himself with Cleopatra, had amassed a large fleet to challenge Octavian's control of Rome's eastern provinces. In the end, Octavian's fleet, commanded by his general Agrippa, decisively defeated Antony and Cleopatra's forces.

The defeat of Antony was not only a military victory but also a political one. After the battle, Antony and Cleopatra retreated to Egypt, where they both committed suicide (he with a sword, she with poisonous snakes), leaving Octavian as the undisputed master of the Roman world. The Battle of Actium marked the end of the Roman civil wars and the collapse of the Republic. With no significant rivals left, Octavian stood poised to assume supreme power.

Octavian Becomes Augustus (27 BC)

In 27 BC, Octavian took the final step in his rise to power. He returned to Rome and presented himself not as a monarch, but as the "First Citizen" (Princeps) of Rome. In a dramatic display of republicanism, Octavian offered to relinquish his extraordinary powers. The Senate, however, granted him sweeping authority, including control of the military and the power to appoint provincial governors. Although Octavian maintained the outward forms of the Republic, in reality, he now held unrivaled control over the Roman state.

Augustus Caesar Octavian

The Senate formally awarded Octavian the title Augustus, meaning "the revered one." This title, combined with his new powers, marked the beginning of the Roman Empire. Augustus' reign established the Principate, a new political system where power was concentrated in the hands of one man, but the institutions of the Republic were preserved in form. The Senate remained, but it was now largely ceremonial, and Augustus was the true ruler of Rome.

The Principate System and Pax Romana

The Principate was a system designed to present Augustus as the restorer of the Republic, even though he wielded absolute power. Augustus' careful management of his public image allowed him to maintain the illusion that the Republic was still in place, while in reality, the imperial system was being born. Under Augustus, Rome's borders were secured, and its military strength became unparalleled. He reformed the government, stabilizing the empire and instituting policies that would shape Rome for centuries to come.

One of Augustus' greatest achievements was the establishment of the Pax Romana ("Roman Peace"), a period of relative peace and stability that lasted for over 200 years. Augustus' reforms brought a sense of order to the empire after decades of civil war. He built new infrastructure, including roads, aqueducts, and buildings, which helped integrate the far-flung provinces of the empire. Augustus also reformed the legal system, creating a more uniform set of laws across the empire. The consolidation of power in Augustus' hands marked the end of the Roman Republic and the beginning of a new era in Roman history - the Roman Empire.

Augustus ruled Rome for over 40 years, and under his leadership, Rome transformed from a city-state teetering on the brink of collapse into the dominant power in the Mediterranean world. His reign set the template for future emperors, and his legacy would shape Rome for centuries after his death in 14 AD. The birth of the Roman Empire was not just the end of the Republic, but the dawn of a new world order that would leave an indelible mark on history.

ᴅᴅDID YOU KNOW

- *Augustus was ruling at the time of Jesus Christ's birth and was the person to order the census that took Mary and Joesph to Bethlehem. He is mentioned in the Bible in the Gospel of Luke 2:1.*

PART II: ROME AT ITS HEIGHT

CHAPTER 3: EMPERORS AND POWER – WHO RULED ROME

The Roman Empire, at its height, was ruled by a series of emperors who shaped the world through their ambition, military prowess, and political acumen. Their power, often absolute, was rooted in military control, the loyalty of the legions, and a system of governance that blended monarchy and republican forms. This chapter explores the key imperial dynasties and the nature of power in the Roman Empire, examining the Julio-Claudian and Flavian dynasties, the "Five Good Emperors," and the Severan dynasty, alongside the later division of the Empire and the emperors' complex roles as both military commanders and divine figures.

The Julio-Claudian Dynasty (Augustus to Nero)

The Julio-Claudian dynasty, the first imperial family to hold sway over the Roman world, spanned from Augustus (27 BC–14 AD) to Nero (54–68 AD). This family set the template for imperial rule, blending the remnants of the Republic's political institutions with autocratic power. Their rule, marked by triumph and tragedy, laid the foundations for the Roman Empire, but it also revealed the inherent instability and danger of absolute power.

Augustus (63 BC – 14 AD), the first emperor, crafted a political system that maintained the appearance of republican governance, but in reality, he held supreme authority. His reign ushered in the Pax Romana, a period of relative peace and prosperity that would last for over 200 years. Augustus' reign was marked by extensive reforms, a reorganization of the army, and the creation of the imperial bureaucracy. Despite his vast power, Augustus skillfully presented himself as the first among equals, always claiming to be serving the people and the Senate.

Augustus' successor was his adopted stepson, Tiberius (42 BC – 37 AD), who ruled for 23 years. This set a precedent for future emperors to choose their successors through adoption, rather than biological inheritance. He was competent but increasingly paranoid and withdrawn. His reign saw little major military conflict, but political intrigue and purges marked the latter years of his rule. Tiberius' retirement to the island of Capri, leaving the administration in the hands of his Praetorian Prefect Sejanus, led to further instability and corruption.

Following Tiberius came his grand-nephew, Gaius Julius Caesar Augustus Germanicus, better known as Caligula (12 – 41 AD). Caligula's ascent to power was unexpected. After the death of Tiberius in 37 AD, the Praetorian Guard, the imperial bodyguard, played a crucial role in ensuring Caligula's succession. Despite having other potential heirs, the Praetorians saw Caligula as a figure they could control and manipulate.

16th-century bust of Caligula

At the age of 24, he began his reign with widespread popularity but soon descended into erratic cruelty and excess. He's generally accepted as Rome's worst emperor, causing famine and draining the Roman treasury in building vast monuments to his own greatness. His behavior alienated the Senate, and after just four years, he was assassinated by members of the Senate and his own guard.

ooDID YOU KNOW

- *Caligula earned the nickname "Caligula," meaning "little boot" in Latin, from the soldiers who affectionately called him that during his child-*

hood when he accompanied his father on military campaigns, wearing a miniature military uniform.

- *He engaged in lavish banquets, often inviting his horse Incitatus to dine with him, a gesture that further fueled rumors about his erratic behavior.*

Claudius (10 BC – 54 AD) followed Caligula's reign, and though initially seen as weak and unlikely, he proved to be an able administrator and military leader. Claudius expanded the empire by conquering Britain in 43 AD and oversaw the creation of important infrastructure, such as the Ostian Port and the expansion of the road network. Claudius, however, was marred by personal and political intrigue, particularly involving his wives and his eventual poisoning by his last wife, Agrippina the Younger (who was also his niece!).

The last of the Julio-Claudian emperors, Nero (37–68 AD), began his reign, at the age of 16, with reforms and general popularity, but soon became infamous for his indulgence in luxury, cruelty, and tyrannical behavior. . His early reign was influenced heavily by his mother, Agrippina, who sought to maintain control over the young emperor. His was also influenced by his tutor, the philosopher Seneca, and the Praetorian Prefect Burrus, who provided stability.

One of the most infamous incidents of Nero's reign was the murder of his mother, Agrippina, in 59 AD, and his persecution of Christians. The Great Fire of Rome in 64 AD, which Nero was rumored to have started or at least failed to stop, further tarnished his reputation. Eventually, facing revolts and military discontent, Nero fled Rome, but facing imminent capture and execution, Nero chose to take his own life. He died by stabbing himself in the throat with the assistance of his private secretary, Epaphroditos – he was just 30 years old. His death marked the end of the Julio-Claudian dynasty.

⬜⬜DID YOU KNOW

- *The Pisonian Conspiracy of 65 - 66 AD reflected the widespread discontent with Nero's rule and the desire for a change in leadership. They plotted to assassinate Nero and replace him with Piso as the new emperor. However, the conspiracy was exposed before it could be fully executed. Many involved, including Seneca, were implicated and forced to commit suicide.*

- *One of the most infamous incidents of Nero's reign was the murder of his mother, Agrippina, in 59 AD. Tensions had arisen between Nero and Agrippina, and Nero ordered her assassination, reflecting the strain within the imperial family.*

The Flavians and the Five Good Emperors

After the fall of the Julio-Claudian dynasty, Rome entered a period of instability, known as the Year of the Four Emperors (69 AD), in which civil war and competition for power raged. In this time, Galba, aged 70, ruled for seven months, before being assassinated by his successor's supporters. He was followed by Otho, who at 36 years old, reigned for an even shorter time – just three months! He committed suicide after defeat at the Battle of Bedriacum. Vetellius, aged 54, followed, reigning for 8 months, until his defeat in battle with his successor, Vespasian. He was executed in Rome by Vespasian's soldiers on December 20. It had been quite a tumultuous, and bloody year!

So, Vespasian (9–79 AD) emerged victorious and founded the Flavian dynasty. His reign, and that of his sons Titus (79–81 AD) and Domitian (81–96 AD), was marked by military victories, rebuilding efforts, and harsh but effective rule.

17th century marble bust of Vespasian

Vespasian, having risen from the ranks of the army, stabilized Rome and secured the empire. His most notable achievement was the Flavian Amphitheatre, the iconic Colosseum, in Rome, which became the stage for gladiatorial games and entertainment for the masses.

▫▫DID YOU KNOW

- *Before his ascension to the imperial throne, Vespasian played a crucial role in the Roman-Jewish War (66–73 AD). As a general, he conducted the Siege of Jerusalem in 70 CE, culminating in the destruction of the Second Temple.*

- *Vespasian initiated several construction projects aimed at revitalizing Rome. The most famous among them was the construction of the Flavian Amphitheatre, known as the Colosseum. Starting at around 70 AD, it took around 10 years to build the Coliseum, over the demolished palaces of Nero, and could hold up to 80,000 spectators.*

- *It has been estimated that 500,000 people and more than 1 million animals died in the Coliseum, Rome's great gladiatorial arena.*

Vespasian's reign set the tone for his sons, though Titus, his successor, was widely respected for his handling of the eruption of Mount Vesuvius in 79 AD and the destruction of Pompeii and Herculaneum. Titus also oversaw the completion of the Colosseum and military triumphs in Judea.

Domitian, however, took a more authoritarian approach, positioning himself as a god and ruling with autocratic power. His reign was marked by military success and extensive building projects, but also by political purges and executions of rivals. Domitian's rule ended with his assassination in 96 AD, which brought an end to the Flavian dynasty.

With Domitian's death, the Senate took control of the empire and sought a more cooperative approach to governance, ushering in the era of the "Five Good Emperors". These emperors — Nerva (96–98 AD), Trajan (98–117 AD), Hadrian (117–138 AD), Antoninus Pius (138–161 AD), and Marcus Aurelius (161–180 AD) — presided over an era of stability and prosperity. Under their rule, the empire reached its greatest territorial extent and enjoyed a period of relative peace and good governance.

- Hadrian focused on consolidating and fortifying the empire's borders, notably constructing Hadrian's Wall in Britain.

- Antoninus Pius was known for his peaceful reign and administrative reforms.

- Marcus Aurelius, the philosopher-emperor, faced numerous military challenges but is best remembered for his Stoic writings, especially his work, Meditations.

Despite the successes of the Five Good Emperors, the succession crisis that followed Marcus Aurelius' death in 180 AD would begin the decline of the empire, with a series of less capable emperors weakening the imperial system.

Marcus Aurelius

▫▫DID YOU KNOW

- *During Trajan's reign (98 – 117 AD) the Empire reached its greatest geographical extent. It was possible to travel from Britain to the Persian Gulf without leaving Roman territory. And of course, Rome controlled all the Mediterranean coastline.*

- *At its height the Roman Empire covered 40 modern nations and 5 million square km.*

- *In 122 AD Hadrian ordered the building of a wall in Britain 'to separate*

Romans from barbarians'. The wall was about 73 miles long and up to 10 feet high. Built of stone with regular forts and customs posts, it is an extraordinary achievement and parts of it still survive.

The Severan Dynasty and the Rise of Military Influence

The Severan dynasty (193–235 AD) began with Septimius Severus, who came to power after the assassination of Commodus, the son of Marcus Aurelius. The Severans were known for their military strength, with Severus and his successors relying heavily on the support of the army. The dynasty saw the expansion of the empire into parts of Africa and the Middle East, including a campaign against the Parthian Empire, which saw temporary Roman victories in Mesopotamia.

During this period, the army grew in influence, and emperors increasingly relied on military support to secure their rule. Carus, Carinus, and Numerian were later emperors who ruled during a time of civil war and instability, but their reigns showed the growing militarization of the empire. Military commanders were able to rise to imperial power with the support of their legions, further cementing the army's role in Roman politics.

Later Emperors and the Division of the Empire

The latter days of the Roman Empire saw a steady decline in the unity of the empire. A combination of external pressures (barbarian invasions), internal unrest, and economic challenges led to the eventual division of the empire. The most significant moment came with the reign of Diocletian (284–305 AD), who divided the empire into the Eastern and Western Roman Empires in an attempt to improve administrative efficiency and military defense.

Diocletian's reforms included the creation of the Tetrarchy - a system of rule by four emperors, two in the East and two in the West - to prevent civil wars over succession. Despite the initial success of this system, the Roman Empire would continue to fracture, eventually leading to the establishment of the Byzantine Empire in the East and the fall of the Western Roman Empire in 476 AD.

Emperors as Military Commanders, Gods, and Administrators

Roman emperors were unique in that they held roles as both military commanders and administrators. Their power was built on the loyalty of the legions, who often made or broke emperors. Emperors commanded the army directly, and their legitimacy was deeply tied to their military successes and their ability to maintain peace and security.

In addition to their military authority, emperors were often seen as semi-divine figures. The practice of imperial cult worship began with Augustus, who was deified after his death, and continued throughout the empire. Emperors were worshipped as gods, and their image was propagated throughout the empire in statues, coins, and temples. This fusion of military, political, and religious power made emperors central to Roman identity and governance.

CHAPTER 4: A WORLD EMPIRE – SIZE, PROVINCES, AND BORDERS

The Roman Empire at its height was a world-spanning behemoth, stretching from the misty hills of Britain in the northwest to the sun-drenched deserts of Egypt in the southeast, and from the Atlantic shores of Spain to the ancient kingdoms of Syria and Mesopotamia in the east. This vast expanse of land was more than just a territorial conquest; it was a complex network of provinces, people, and cultures, all held together by the power of Rome and its remarkable ability to govern and integrate diverse territories.

In this chapter, we explore how Rome expanded its empire, governed its vast provinces, and managed the borders of its world-spanning empire. From the famed Hadrian's Wall in the north to the Euphrates in the east, we will see how Rome shaped the landscape of the ancient world and forged a multicultural empire that would have a profound influence on the course of history.

Mapping the Empire: From Britain to Egypt, Spain to Syria

At its peak, the Roman Empire covered over 5 million square kilometers, making it one of the largest empires in history. Its boundaries stretched from the cold, windswept islands of Britannia (modern-day Britain) to the deserts of Egypt, from the misty forests of Germania to the rolling plains of North Africa. The empire encompassed a staggering array of geographic features, cultures, and climates, each posing unique challenges to Roman governance, military control, and cultural integration.

The Roman Empire at its peak

The Western Provinces: Britain, Gaul, Spain, and North Africa

In the West, the empire expanded across the Mediterranean basin and into the fringes of Europe. Britannia was a key conquest under the emperor Claudius in 43 AD, though Rome had made earlier attempts to control the island. The Romans built roads, forts, and towns across Britain, and their influence can still be seen in the remnants of Hadrian's Wall, which marked the northern frontier of Roman Britain.

□□DID YOU KNOW

- *When the Roman soldiers were first ordered to invade Britain in 43 AD, they went on strike on the grounds that it was beyond the known world and there could even be monsters.*

To the south, Gaul (modern-day France) was another major conquest, brought under Roman control after Julius Caesar's campaigns during the Gallic Wars (58–50 BC). Gaul's rich farmland and strategic position made it a valuable province. The region would later become an important center for trade and culture, blending Roman law, language, and customs with native traditions.

Hispania (modern Spain and Portugal) was fully integrated into the empire after a series of military campaigns, with Tarraco (modern Tarragona) becoming the seat of Roman governance in the region. Spain's mineral wealth, particularly silver, played a crucial role in sustaining the empire's economy.

In North Africa, the Roman provinces of Africa Proconsularis (modern Tunisia, western Libya, and Algeria) were rich in agricultural resources, especially grain, which fed Rome and other parts of the empire. The famous city of Carthage, once Rome's bitter rival, was rebuilt and became a thriving metropolis under Roman rule.

The Eastern Provinces: Syria, Judea, and Egypt

In the East, the Roman Empire came into contact with some of the oldest and most advanced civilizations of the ancient world. Syria and Judea were strategic provinces, providing access to trade routes and rich agricultural land. The province of Judea would become especially important due to its religious significance and the rise of Christianity, which would later spread throughout the empire.

Egypt was a jewel in the Roman crown. After the defeat of Cleopatra and Mark Antony at the Battle of Actium in 31 BC, Egypt became a Roman province. It was not only a source of wealth, especially grain, but also a cultural crossroads between Greek, Egyptian, and Roman traditions. Alexandria, one of the empire's most important cities, was a center of learning, philosophy, and commerce.

How Rome Governed Its Provinces: Governors, Legions, and Local Elites

Roman governance of its vast empire was a delicate balance of military control, administrative efficiency, and cooperation with local elites. Each province was ruled by a governor, a Roman official who was often a former consul or general.

Governors had wide-ranging powers, overseeing both civil administration and military matters.

The key to maintaining Roman control was the legions, elite Roman soldiers stationed throughout the empire to protect its borders, enforce Roman law, and quell rebellions. The legions were not only military forces but also symbols of Roman authority. They built roads, forts, and towns, and helped to integrate the empire by imposing Roman law and customs.

However, the Romans knew that brute force alone could not maintain control over such a vast empire. They were pragmatic rulers, willing to work with the local elites in the provinces. In many cases, local rulers were allowed to retain some degree of power in exchange for loyalty to Rome. This system of client kings and local magistrates helped ensure that Roman control was not seen as an occupying force but rather as part of the local political fabric.

Frontiers: Hadrian's Wall, the Danube, the Euphrates

One of the defining features of the Roman Empire was its carefully defined borders. While the empire expanded across three continents, there were always areas of uncertainty and conflict at the empire's fringes. The Romans constructed extensive systems of fortifications and defensive walls to protect their borders and maintain their imperial integrity.

Hadrian's Wall, built under the emperor Hadrian in the second century AD, marked the northernmost boundary of Roman Britain, stretching across the island from the Solway Firth to the Tyne River. The wall was about 73 miles long and up to 10 feet high, built of stone with regular forts and customs posts.

A section of Hadrian's Wall in northern England

The wall was a symbol of Roman military power and an important physical barrier between the civilized world of Rome and the unknown, hostile territories to the north.

Further south, the Danube River marked the border between Roman territory and the wild lands of the Germanic tribes. The river itself was a natural defense, and the Romans built a series of forts along its banks to secure the frontier. The Euphrates River, in the east, separated the Roman Empire from the rival Parthian Empire. The Romans never fully conquered the region to the east of the Euphrates but fought a series of wars with the Parthians and their successor states, including the Sassanids.

These frontiers were not static but areas of constant movement and conflict. While the Romans sought to secure their borders, they also engaged in military campaigns to push these boundaries further, sometimes through negotiation, sometimes through war.

Multicultural Rome – Integration of Conquered Peoples

One of Rome's greatest achievements was its ability to integrate a vast array of peoples and cultures into the empire. The Roman approach to cultural assimilation was pragmatic, recognizing the value of local customs and traditions while imposing Roman law and governance.

In Gaul, for instance, Romanization involved the construction of Roman-style towns, roads, and baths, while the local Celtic tribes adopted Roman language, dress, and architecture. The Roman colony system, which established Roman citizens in newly conquered territories, encouraged the spread of Roman culture and provided a loyal base of support.

In Egypt, Roman rule was more administratively structured but still incorporated local Egyptian customs. The cult of Isis continued to thrive, and Egyptian art and religion were integrated into Roman life. Likewise, in Syria, local gods and traditions were respected, and many cities retained a degree of autonomy under Roman governance.

In the eastern provinces, the Romans often adopted local leaders and military structures, offering them Roman citizenship in exchange for loyalty. This system helped maintain peace and allowed for a more peaceful integration of conquered peoples.

The Complexity of Roman Imperialism

The Roman Empire's vast size, complex governance, and multicultural integration were essential to its long-lasting success. By building a system of roads, fortifications, and colonies, the Romans ensured that their empire was connected and unified. Their ability to govern through a mix of military might and cooperation with local elites allowed them to manage diverse populations, cultures, and landscapes.

The Roman Empire was, in many ways, a model for future empires in terms of territorial control, military strategy, and cultural integration. While it ultimately succumbed to internal strife and external pressures, the legacy of Roman imperialism, its systems of governance, law, and infrastructure, has endured through the ages.

In the next chapter, we will delve into how Rome built its military might and conquered vast territories, shaping the course of history through its legions, tactics, and engineering innovations.

CHAPTER 5: LEGIONS AND CONQUEST – HOW ROME WON AN EMPIRE

Rome's empire was built on the backs of its legions, disciplined, efficient, and unyielding in battle. The Roman army was more than just a fighting force; it was a symbol of Rome's dominance, a tool of empire-building that enabled the expansion and consolidation of Roman power across three continents. This chapter explores the inner workings of the Roman military machine, the strategies and tactics that fueled Roman conquests, and the engineering feats that supported Rome's dominance. We will also examine some of the most notable military campaigns, from Julius Caesar's conquest of Gaul to the campaigns of Trajan in Dacia and Mesopotamia, and the final push into Britain.

The Structure of the Roman Army: Legions, Centurions, Auxiliaries

The Roman army's strength lay in its organization. The backbone of the army was the legion, a flexible and well-organized fighting unit that could be deployed in various formations and adapted to different combat situations. A legion typically consisted of around 5,000 soldiers, though the number could fluctuate depending on the needs of the campaign. The legions were divided into cohorts (approximately 500 men each), and within each cohort, soldiers were further grouped into smaller units, the centuries (roughly 80 men), commanded by a centurion.

Centurions were the backbone of the Roman army's leadership. They were responsible for maintaining discipline, ensuring training, and leading their men into battle. Centurions were not appointed based on aristocratic birth but by merit, and many rose through the ranks due to their leadership abilities and combat prowess. It was their ability to inspire loyalty and discipline in their soldiers that was key to Rome's military success.

While the legionaries formed the heart of the Roman army, the auxiliaries were equally important. These were non-citizen troops who came from the provinces and various allied nations. The auxiliaries provided vital support, particularly in specialized areas such as cavalry, archery, and light infantry. As they were not Roman citizens initially, they were promised Roman citizenship as a reward for their service. The auxiliary troops added flexibility and strength to the army, allowing it to be effective in diverse environments.

Strategies and Tactics of Conquest

Roman military success was built on a combination of superior strategy, disciplined training, and tactical flexibility. The Roman legions were renowned for their ability to fight in close formations, making them an almost unstoppable force in battle. But the Romans were also masters of adaptability, adjusting their tactics to suit the terrain and the enemy they faced.

One of the most famous tactics employed by the Romans was the testudo or "tortoise" formation, where soldiers would form a dense shield wall on all sides and overhead, protecting themselves from missiles and enabling them to advance slowly and steadily against enemy fortifications.

The Romans also utilized siege warfare to great effect. They were expert builders of siege engines, such as ballistae (giant crossbows) and onagers (a type of catapult), which allowed them to breach the walls of even the most fortified cities. Roman engineers would quickly construct temporary siege works, like battering rams and towers, to facilitate their advance. The use of military roads also played a vital role in Roman military logistics, allowing the legions to move quickly and strike deep into enemy territory.

Another key to Roman military success was the integration of conquered peoples into the Roman army. By recruiting soldiers from the regions they conquered, the Romans were able to build a vast and diverse military force. This approach not only helped secure their control over vast territories but also ensured that Romanization, the spread of Roman culture, law, and customs, permeated throughout the empire.

Engineering and Logistics: Roads, Forts, and Supply Chains

The Roman military was not just about soldiers fighting on the battlefield, it was also about efficient logistics and infrastructure that supported those soldiers. The Romans were master engineers, and their military success was often as much about their ability to build roads, forts, and supply chains as it was about battlefield tactics.

Roman roads were among the most advanced and durable in the ancient world. Constructed with layers of stone, gravel, and paving stones, these roads allowed the legions to march quickly across the empire. The Via Appia, known as the "Queen of Roads", connected Rome to southern Italy, and the Via Augusta ran through Spain. These roads were not just vital for military movement; they also facilitated trade, communication, and the spread of Roman culture.

Roman forts (or castra) were constructed at regular intervals along the roads to provide shelter, rest, and protection for the army. These forts were designed to be self-sustaining, with barracks, kitchens, latrines, and storage facilities. Many of the forts were strategically placed to control key locations and act as bases for Roman expansion.

Supply chains were another critical component of Roman military logistics. The legions needed a constant flow of food, equipment, and reinforcements, and the Romans developed an intricate system of supply depots and distribution networks to ensure that their soldiers were always well-equipped and fed.

ɒɒDID YOU KNOW

- *"All roads lead to Rome" is more than a saying — the Romans revolutionized road building. Unlike earlier civilizations, they paved their roads: 10 feet deep, layered with stone, sand, gravel, and capped with volcanic rock. Built to be straight, durable, and long-lasting, many still form the basis of Europe's highways today, with the Appian Way as the most famous example.*

The Great Wars of Rome – Conquest, Crisis, and Glory

Rome's story is one of wars, great, grinding, and world-changing wars. From its earliest struggles for survival to the vast campaigns that brought emperors fame and enemies to ruin, Rome's history was written on the battlefield. The Republic and Empire alike were forged, expanded, and sometimes almost broken by conflicts against rivals who, in their time, seemed as mighty as Rome itself. These wars were not fought merely for territory, but for prestige, survival, and the Roman vision of order in the world. Here, we trace some of the greatest, epic struggles that defined an empire.

The Punic Wars (264–146 BC) - Rome vs. Carthage – The Mediterranean Decided

If one set of wars made Rome the dominant power of the Mediterranean, it was the three Punic Wars. Carthage, a rich North African city-state founded by the Phoenicians, was Rome's great rival for maritime and commercial supremacy.

The First Punic War (264–241 BC) began over control of Sicily. Rome, a land power with little naval experience, built a fleet from scratch, adding the corvus, a boarding bridge, to turn sea battles into infantry fights. After two decades of grinding warfare, Carthage sued for peace, ceding Sicily, the first Roman province outside Italy.

The Second Punic War (218–201 BC) is remembered for one man: Hannibal Barca. In one of the most audacious moves in military history, Hannibal marched an army, including war elephants, from New Carthage (modern-day Cartagena in Spain) crossing the Pyrenees and over the Alps into Italy. Victories at Trebia, Lake Trasimene, and Cannae shook Rome to its core. Yet Rome refused to surrender. Under Quintus Fabius Maximus, the "Cunctator" (Delayer), and later Publius Cornelius Scipio Africanus, Rome adapted, striking at Carthage's holdings in Spain before invading Africa. At the Battle of Zama (202 BC), Scipio defeated Hannibal, ending the war and making Rome master of the western Mediterranean.

Hannibal Barca

The Third Punic War (149–146 BC) was a short, brutal siege. Rome, determined to eliminate Carthage forever, destroyed the city, enslaved its people, and symbolically cursed the land. The phrase "Carthago delenda est" ("Carthage must be destroyed") became reality.

ooDID YOU KNOW

- *The Battle of Cape Ecnomus in 256 BC during the First Punic War is considered one of the largest naval battles in history. It involved a combined total of around 680 warships and around 290,000 combatants.*

- *Hannibal's crossing of the Alps took place in the Second Punic War in 218 BC. He took 38,000 infantry, 8,000 cavalry and 38 elephants into the mountains and down into Italy.*

- *At the Battle of Cannae in 216 BC, Hannibal inflicted on Rome the worst defeat in its military history. Between 50,000 and 70,000 Roman soldiers were killed or captured by a much smaller force. It is considered one of the great military triumphs (and disasters) in history, the perfect 'battle of annihilation'.*

- *At Lake Trasimene in 217 BC, Hannibal lured the Roman army under Flaminius into a narrow lakeside pass, then sprung a massive ambush with troops hidden in the hills. In just a few hours, the Romans were surrounded and annihilated, with tens of thousands killed or captured, making it history's largest ambush and a stunning example of Hannibal's genius.*

The Macedonian and Hellenistic Wars (215–148 BC) - Rome in the East

While fighting Carthage, Rome also became entangled in Greece and the eastern Mediterranean. The Macedonian kings, successors to Alexander the Great, sought advantage in Rome's distractions. After a series of Macedonian Wars, Rome dismantled the kingdom of Macedon and defeated the Seleucid Empire at Magnesia (190 BC), opening the way for dominance over Greece and Asia Minor. By 148 BC, Macedonia was a Roman province, and Greece followed soon after.

The Conquest of Gaul (58–50 BC) - Julius Caesar's Masterstroke

Few campaigns in Roman history were as dramatic, or as politically consequential, as Julius Caesar's conquest of Gaul. Officially, Caesar's task was to protect Roman allies from migrating tribes like the Helvetii. In reality, Caesar was building a personal power base.

Over eight years, Caesar crushed Gallic coalitions, defeated the Germanic king Ariovistus, and crossed into Britain in expeditions that, while limited, expanded Rome's reach. The climax came in 52 BC at Alesia, where Caesar besieged Vercingetorix, the charismatic Gallic leader. Using vast fortifications to encircle the enemy while defending against a relief force, Caesar won a decisive victory.

Gaul became a Roman province, enriching Caesar, and setting the stage for civil war in Rome.

Rome's Civil Wars (88–30 BC) - Republic in Turmoil

As Rome grew richer, politics grew bloodier. Personal ambition, military loyalty to commanders over the Senate, and social unrest led to a century of internal conflict.

The Marius–Sulla Conflict (88–82 BC) began when Lucius Cornelius Sulla marched his legions on Rome, a shocking first in Roman history, after a dispute with his rival Gaius Marius. This set a dangerous precedent: that generals could seize power by force.

Caesar vs. Pompey (49–45 BC) was the most famous civil war. After the Gallic conquest, the Senate, led by Pompey, ordered Caesar to disband his army. Instead, he crossed the Rubicon River, declaring, "Alea iacta est" ("The die is cast"). Caesar's swift campaign drove Pompey to Greece, where Caesar triumphed at Pharsalus (48 BC). Pompey fled to Egypt, where he was murdered. Caesar emerged as Rome's ruler, only to be assassinated in 44 BC.

Pompey the Great

The Final War of the Republic (32–30 BC) pitted Octavian (Caesar's adopted heir) against Mark Antony and Cleopatra VII of Egypt. The decisive moment came at the Battle of Actium (31 BC), a naval engagement where Octavian's admiral, Agrippa, outmaneuvered Antony's forces. Antony and Cleopatra took their own lives, leaving Octavian as sole ruler, soon to be Augustus, the first emperor.

ooDID YOU KNOW

- *Pompey was murdered in Egypt by Egyptian court officials. When his head and seal were presented to Caesar, the last standing member of the triumvirate is said to have wept. He had the conspirators executed.*

The Dacian Wars (101–102, 105–106 AD) - Trajan's Eastern Triumph

Under Emperor Trajan, Rome reached its greatest territorial extent. The wealthy kingdom of Dacia (modern Romania), ruled by King Decebalus, had long been a thorn in Rome's side. Trajan's two campaigns were monumental in scale, involving massive engineering works such as the Danube Bridge. In 106 CE, Dacia was annexed as a province, its gold mines enriching Rome. Trajan celebrated with the famous Trajan's Column, its spiral reliefs chronicling the wars.

Rome in the East – The Parthian and Mesopotamian Campaigns

The Parthian Empire, a powerful state in Persia, was one of Rome's most persistent foes. In 53 BC, the Roman general Crassus suffered a catastrophic defeat at Carrhae, where Parthian horse archers and cataphracts (heavily armored cavalry) annihilated his legions. Later emperors sought revenge: Trajan briefly conquered Mesopotamia in 116 AD, but the territory proved impossible to hold. The Parthians, and later their Sassanian successors, remained Rome's eastern rivals for centuries.

The Conquest of Britain (43–84 AD) - Rome's Island Frontier

Julius Caesar had raided Britain in 55–54 BC, but it was Emperor Claudius who ordered the full-scale invasion in 43 AD. The legions pushed north and west, building roads and forts, but resistance was fierce. The most famous uprising was led by Boudica, queen of the Iceni, in 60–61 AD. After her defeat, Roman power reached as far as modern Scotland, where Agricola fought the Caledonians at Mons Graupius (83 AD). Hadrian's Wall, built in the 120s AD, marked the empire's northern limit.

Jewish–Roman Wars (66–135 AD) - Faith and Empire Collide

Religion and politics combined explosively in Judea. The First Jewish Revolt (66–73 AD) saw rebels seize Jerusalem. Vespasian's son Titus besieged and captured the city in 70 AD, destroying the Second Temple, a defining event in Jewish history. Later revolts, including the Bar Kokhba uprising (132–135 AD), were brutally crushed, and many Jews were dispersed across the empire.

Rome's Germanic Wars

Rome's northern frontier was always dangerous. In 9 AD, three legions under Publius Quinctilius Varus were ambushed and annihilated by Arminius, a Germanic chieftain, in the Teutoburg Forest. This disaster ended Rome's ambitions to conquer Germania east of the Rhine. Later emperors campaigned there, but the frontier remained a zone of constant tension.

The Marcomannic Wars (166–180 AD) - Marcus Aurelius on the Danube

Under Marcus Aurelius, philosopher and emperor, Rome faced massive invasions by Germanic and Sarmatian tribes along the Danube. Years of campaigning pushed them back, but the wars drained manpower and foreshadowed the pressures that would later overwhelm the empire.

Rebellions and Resistance: Boudica, Jewish Revolts, and Germanic Tribes

No empire can expand without facing resistance, and the Roman Empire was no exception. Rebellions and uprisings were a constant threat to Roman rule, but they were also a testament to the strength and resilience of the people who resisted Roman domination.

Boudica's Revolt (60–61 AD) was one of the most famous uprisings against Roman rule in Britain. Boudica, queen of the Iceni tribe, led a massive rebellion against the Romans after the mistreatment of her people. She destroyed Roman cities, including Camulodunum (modern-day Colchester), and inflicted heavy casualties on the Roman legions. However, her forces were ultimately defeated at the Battle of Watling Street, and Boudica's revolt was crushed. Despite her defeat, Boudica became a symbol of resistance and a lasting figure in British history.

Statue of Boadica in London

The Jewish Revolts in the eastern provinces were another significant source of unrest. The first revolt (66–73 AD) led to the destruction of the Second Temple in Jerusalem and the eventual defeat of the Jews by the Romans. The second revolt, the Bar Kokhba Revolt (132–136 AD), was an even more intense resistance movement, ultimately crushed by Emperor Hadrian. The Romans responded with brutal measures, and the Jewish population was largely dispersed.

The Germanic tribes were another ongoing threat. They resisted Roman expansion and posed a serious military challenge, especially in the regions north of the Danube. The famous Battle of the Teutoburg Forest (9 AD), in which three Roman legions were ambushed and destroyed by an alliance of Germanic tribes, was a devastating setback for Rome and highlighted the difficulties of conquering the Germanic territories.

The Legacy of Roman Military Conquest

The Roman legions were the backbone of Rome's power, enabling the empire to conquer vast territories and maintain control over a diverse range of cultures and peoples. The army's discipline, tactical genius, and strategic foresight were key factors in Rome's expansion. Yet, the Roman army was also a symbol of the empire's ability to integrate and assimilate, creating a multicultural empire that would leave a lasting legacy on the world.

Through conquest, diplomacy, and a well-developed infrastructure, the Romans created an empire that lasted for centuries. But the empire's military might would eventually face challenges that even the greatest generals could not overcome.

CHAPTER 6. THE CITIES OF THE ROMAN EMPIRE – JEWELS OF STONE AND MARBLE

At its height, the Roman Empire was not merely a collection of provinces, but a network of cities, some ancient, some newly built, bound together by roads, law, and commerce. They were the lifeblood of imperial power, centers where the authority of Rome was made visible in stone and marble, where trade thrived, and where citizens and subjects alike participated in the shared rituals of Roman life. From the teeming streets of the capital to frontier outposts, each city told a part of the Empire's story.

Rome – The Eternal City

Rome was the beating heart of the empire, both politically and symbolically. Founded, according to legend, in 753 BC by Romulus, the city grew from a collection of huts on the Palatine Hill into the largest urban centre of the ancient world, with a population possibly exceeding a million by the 2nd century AD.

The city was both a marvel and a challenge. Its streets bustled with senators in togas, traders hawking wares from across the empire, and the urban poor living in multi-storey insulae (apartment blocks). Rome's monumental core reflected its role as capital: the Forum, the Senate House, the Colosseum for gladiatorial combat, the Circus Maximus for chariot races, and countless temples dedicated to the Roman gods.

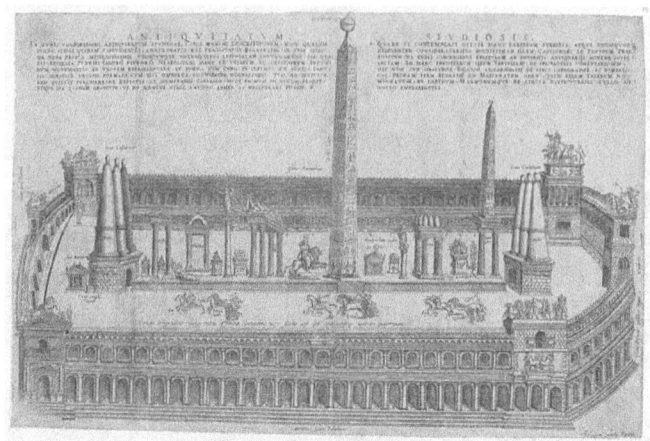

Circus Maximus

As the seat of the emperor, Rome was the ultimate prize in politics, with control of the city meaning control of the empire. It was also a cultural magnet, drawing in architects, artists, and thinkers from all provinces. The city's aqueducts, paved roads, and sewage system were engineering feats unmatched in the ancient world, ensuring its role as the model for Roman urban planning.

▫▫DID YOU KNOW

- *The Circus Maximus, largely dedicated to chariot racing, held crowds of up to 250,000, a quarter of Rome's population at the time! Beginning around 50 BC, Julius Caesar and Augustus, the first Emperor, helped develop it from a simple racing track to the largest stadium in the world.*

Pompeii and Herculaneum – Cities Frozen in Time

Few cities tell us as much about daily Roman life as Pompeii and Herculaneum, thanks to the catastrophic eruption of Mount Vesuvius in 79 AD.

Pompeii, a bustling port and market town, had a population of around 11,000 and was famous for its wealth, villas, and vibrant street life. Its streets reveal a thriving commercial hub, with bakeries, taverns, and bathhouses. Colourful frescoes adorned elite homes, while public buildings like the amphitheatre and basilica reflected both leisure and administration. The eruption buried the city under a thick layer of ash, preserving everyday objects from bread loaves to graffiti.

Pompeii

Herculaneum, smaller but wealthier, lay closer to Vesuvius. Buried under a denser layer of volcanic material, it preserved two-storey houses, wooden furniture, and even papyrus scrolls in the Villa of the Papyri. While Pompeii shows us a bustling middle-class city, Herculaneum offers a glimpse into elite coastal luxury.

Today, these cities remain archaeological treasures, giving us a vivid snapshot of life on an ordinary day in the empire, moments before disaster struck.

Ostia and Portus – Rome's Gateway to the World

Ostia, Rome's first harbour, lay at the mouth of the River Tiber. Founded in the 4th century BC, it was initially a military outpost but evolved into the main port of entry for grain, oil, and other goods feeding the capital's enormous population.

When Ostia's harbour became too small for Rome's needs, the emperors Claudius and Trajan built Portus nearby, a massive artificial harbour with hexagonal basins and deep docks capable of handling the largest merchant ships. Together, Ostia and Portus were Rome's economic arteries, ensuring the city's survival and prosperity.

Ostia itself grew into a lively town of warehouses, markets, temples, and apartment blocks. Its well-preserved mosaics still tell the story of the trades and guilds that kept Rome supplied.

Carthage – Phoenix of the Mediterranean

Once the capital of the Carthaginian Empire and bitter enemy of Rome in the Punic Wars, Carthage was destroyed in 146 BC and famously "ploughed with salt" (though this is likely more myth than fact). Yet Rome rebuilt it a century later as Colonia Julia Carthago, and it became the wealthiest city in Roman Africa.

By the 2nd century AD, Carthage was a hub of trade and learning, exporting grain, olives, and garum (fish sauce) across the empire. Its great amphitheatre, aqueducts, and baths reflected Roman grandeur, while its harbours bustled with Mediterranean commerce. Carthage was also a centre of early Christianity, producing figures such as Tertullian and Cyprian.

Timgad – Rome's African Colony

Founded by Emperor Trajan around 100 AD in modern Algeria, Timgad was a textbook example of Roman colonial planning. Its streets followed a perfect grid, centred on a forum and flanked by a theatre, library, and baths. Nicknamed the "Pompeii of North Africa," Timgad was built for veterans of the Roman army and embodied the imperial goal of Romanising frontier regions.

Timgad's strategic location allowed Rome to control the surrounding Berber tribes and secure the North African grain supply. Its impressive ruins still showcase the precision of Roman urban design.

Timgad symbolised the spread of Roman urban ideals to the edges of the Empire. The town was not just a military outpost, it was a statement that Rome's order and culture could flourish even in remote North Africa.

Leptis Magna – Jewel of Libya

On the Libyan coast, Leptis Magna was transformed from a Phoenician settlement into one of the grandest cities of the Empire, especially under its native son, Emperor Septimius Severus (193–211 AD). He lavished funds on an immense basilica, an ornate arch, and a new harbour.

The city's wealth came from trade in olive oil and exotic goods from Africa's interior. Leptis Magna's remains, with colonnaded streets and marketplaces still standing, give a sense of the ambition and reach of Rome's urban vision.

Leptis Magna

Athens – A Greek City in a Roman World

Although Athens had once been the cultural heart of Greece, by the time Rome conquered it in 146 BC it was politically diminished. Yet under Roman rule, Athens thrived as a center of philosophy, education, and culture. Roman emperors, especially Hadrian, showered it with buildings, including the Library of Hadrian and the completion of the Temple of Olympian Zeus.

For Roman elites, Athens was a place to study rhetoric and philosophy, and the city retained a prestige that was intellectual rather than military. Its theatres still hosted performances, and its ancient monuments were revered by Roman visitors.

Trier – Rome on the Rhine

In the far northwest, Trier (Augusta Treverorum) became one of the most important cities in the later Empire, serving as an imperial capital in the 3rd and 4th centuries AD. From here, emperors governed the turbulent Rhine frontier. The city was endowed with imperial baths, a massive basilica (now a cathedral), and the Porta Nigra, a monumental gate that still stands.

Trier symbolised Rome's adaptability: it could shift the centres of imperial administration to wherever they were most strategically useful.

Ephesus – The Queen of Asia

On the coast of modern Turkey, Ephesus was one of the largest and most prosperous cities in the eastern provinces. Famous for the Temple of Artemis, one of the Seven Wonders of the Ancient World, it also boasted a massive theatre seating 25,000, marble-paved streets, and an impressive library built by Celsus.

Illustration of the Temple of Artemis at Ephesus

As a provincial capital, Ephesus was a hub of commerce, culture, and religion. In the later Empire, it became an important center of early Christianity, visited by Paul the Apostle and mentioned in the Book of Revelation.

Vanished Cities of the East

Some of Rome's eastern cities have left only faint traces. Palmyra in Syria, a caravan city on the desert fringe, flourished as a trading hub between Rome and Persia, blending Greco-Roman and Middle Eastern styles. Dura-Europos, on the Euphrates, was a frontier garrison town with multicultural roots. Petra, in modern Jordan, famed for its rock-cut architecture, became a Roman provincial city after 106 AD but eventually declined as trade routes shifted.

These eastern cities reveal Rome's flexibility in governing and incorporating diverse cultures, from Hellenistic metropolises to desert oases.

Nîmes and Arles – Rome in Southern Gaul

In southern Gaul (modern France), Nîmes (Nemausus) and Arles (Arelate) were showcases of Roman architecture. Nîmes had a beautifully preserved amphitheatre and the Maison Carrée, a pristine Roman temple. Arles boasted an amphitheatre, a theatre, and a circus for chariot racing.

Roman Arena of Nimes

Both cities were centres of trade and administration in the prosperous province of Gallia Narbonensis, and their monuments show how thoroughly Roman culture took root in Gaul.

Roman Britain – Londinium, Verulamium, and Eboracum

In distant Britain, Roman urbanism adapted to a colder, wetter climate. Londinium (London) grew into the provincial capital, with a forum, basilica, and port on the Thames. Verulamium (St Albans) was a major market town, while Eboracum (York) was a key military base and administrative centre. York even hosted emperors, Septimius Severus died there in 211 AD, and Constantine the Great was proclaimed emperor there in 306.

Colchester (Camulodunum) was the first Roman capital of the province and the second-largest city after Londinium. Founded as a colonia for veterans, it boasted a temple to the deified Claudius, which became a rallying point for rebellion during Boudica's uprising in 60 AD. Its strategic location made it a hub for trade and military movement.

Cirencester (Corinium Dobunnorum) grew into the third-largest city in Roman Britain. Surrounded by fertile farmland, it was a centre for wool production and trade. Its basilica and forum reflected its role as an administrative hub, while luxurious townhouses suggest a wealthy local elite.

Roman cities in Britain were fortified with walls, and while they lacked the grandeur of Rome or Carthage, they served as administrative and military anchors on the Empire's farthest frontier.

What Made a Roman City

Wherever they were built, Roman cities shared common features: a central forum, public baths, temples, theatres, and amphitheatres. Streets were laid out in grids when possible, and aqueducts supplied fresh water. These cities were not just places to live, they were statements of Rome's authority, centres for trade, and melting pots for the Empire's diverse peoples.

From the volcanic ruins of Pompeii to the desert splendour of Palmyra, Rome's cities reflected the Empire's scale, diversity, and ambition. They were Rome's most enduring legacy, many still inhabited, their ancient monuments woven into the fabric of modern life.

CHAPTER 7: GREAT ROMANS – MASTERS OF WAR, THOUGHT, AND STATECRAFT AND THEIR ENEMIES

The Makers of Rome's Legacy

The Roman Empire's power and prestige were not merely the product of its institutions, legions, or cities, but of the remarkable individuals who shaped its destiny. From battlefield commanders who carved provinces out of hostile lands, to philosophers whose ideas still echo in modern thought, to writers who captured Rome's triumphs and tragedies, these figures embodied the restless energy, ambition, and adaptability that defined Rome. Some defended the city from annihilation, others expanded it to its greatest borders; some penned works that would inspire centuries; others became the embodiment of Roman virtues and vices alike.

In this chapter, we divide them into three broad groups: Generals and Statesmen, Philosophers and Thinkers, and Enemies Worthy of Rome, for even Rome's adversaries shaped its history, forcing it to adapt, reform, and prove its resilience.

I. Generals and Statesmen

Cincinnatus (c. 519–430 BC) – The Reluctant Dictator

Before Rome was an empire, it was a fragile republic clinging to survival. Lucius Quinctius Cincinnatus, a farmer by trade, became the model of civic virtue. In 458 BC, faced with invasion by the Aequi, Rome called on him to serve as dictator, an emergency office with absolute power. He was called as he had previously served as a Roman consul, one of the two chief executives who ruled the Republic, before retiring from public life to his farm. Within 16 days, he had defeated the enemy, celebrated a triumph, and returned to his plough. In an age when many clung to power, Cincinnatus embodied the ideal of the citizen-soldier, serving the state without personal ambition. His name would echo centuries later, inspiring leaders from George Washington to modern military commanders.

Cincinnatus

Gaius Marius (157–86 BC) – The Military Reformer

Marius revolutionised the Roman army. By opening enlistment to landless citizens and equipping them at the state's expense, he created the first standing, professional legions. His soldiers, the famed Marius' Mules, carried their own supplies, increasing mobility. A seven-time consul, he defended Rome from Germanic invasions and restructured the legions in ways that would endure for centuries. Yet his rivalry with Sulla plunged Rome into civil war.

Lucius Cornelius Sulla (138–78 BC) – The Dictator Who Reshaped the Republic

A ruthless but calculating political operator, Sulla marched his armies on Rome twice, an unprecedented act that shattered the old norms. Victorious in civil war, he took the dictatorship and enacted sweeping constitutional reforms designed to strengthen the Senate and curb the power of popular assemblies. While he retired voluntarily, his example of seizing power by force would echo through Rome's final century as a Republic.

Scipio Africanus (236–183 BC) – The Conqueror of Hannibal

Publius Cornelius Scipio earned the title "Africanus" for his decisive victory over Hannibal at the Battle of Zama in 202 BC, ending the Second Punic War. Brilliant in strategy and charismatic in leadership, he outmanoeuvred Carthage's greatest general, restoring Roman dominance in the western Mediterranean. His campaigns in Spain and Africa transformed Rome into a major imperial power.

Scipio Africanus in the the Naples National Archaeological Museum, 1st century BC

Julius Caesar (100–44 BC) – The General Who Ended the Republic

Few names in history resonate like Caesar's. Brilliant, charismatic, and ruthlessly ambitious, he rose through Rome's turbulent politics to command its armies in Gaul. For nearly a decade, he waged a relentless campaign, conquering a vast territory from the English Channel to the Rhine, defeating the formidable Vercingetorix at Alesia. His Commentaries on the Gallic War not only detailed his victories but also showcased his political genius, written to shape public opinion in Rome.

In 49 BC, Caesar crossed the Rubicon with a single legion, declaring in effect war on the Senate and his rival Pompey. His swift triumph in the ensuing civil war transformed him into dictator for life. He reformed the calendar, expanded citizenship, and overhauled the debt system, but his growing power alarmed the Senate. On the Ides of March, 44 BC, he was stabbed to death by conspirators, a moment that would plunge Rome into further civil war.

Pompey the Great (106–48 BC) – Rome's Eastern Conqueror

Gnaeus Pompeius Magnus — "Pompey the Great" — earned his title young. In his twenties, he earned three triumphs, something unheard of for one so young. He suppressed the pirate menace in the Mediterranean in just three months, restored stability to the Eastern provinces, and defeated Mithridates VI in the East.

Initially an ally of Caesar in the First Triumvirate, Pompey married Caesar's daughter Julia and shared political dominance. But when Julia died and Caesar's power grew, Pompey aligned with the Senate. Their rivalry erupted into civil war, ending with Pompey's defeat at Pharsalus and assassination in Egypt, a tragic end for one of Rome's most celebrated commanders.

Mark Antony (83–30 BC) - Rome's Tragic Contender

Mark Antony began as Caesar's cavalry commander, earning a reputation for bravery and loyalty. After Caesar's assassination, Antony formed the Second Triumvirate with Octavian and Lepidus to crush the assassins. Victory came at Philippi, but Antony's fate was sealed by his alliance with Cleopatra VII of Egypt. Their combined forces were defeated by Octavian at Actium in 31 BC. Facing defeat, Antony and Cleopatra took their own lives, marking the end of the Hellenistic world and Egypt's independence.

Mark Antony and Cleopatra Roman coins

Marcus Vipsanius Agrippa (63–12 BC) – The Emperor's Right Hand

Agrippa was the indispensable man behind Augustus's reign. A master of logistics, engineering, and naval warfare, he secured Octavian's victory at Actium, ending the civil wars. Beyond the battlefield, Agrippa transformed Rome: he rebuilt aqueducts, improved sewers, and commissioned the original Pantheon. Though offered supreme power, he remained loyal to Augustus, shaping the empire from behind the scenes.

Germanicus (15 BC–19 AD) – The People's General

Nephew of Tiberius and adopted father of Caligula, Germanicus was both a war hero and a symbol of hope for the empire. He avenged Rome's catastrophic loss at Teutoburg Forest by recovering the eagles of the lost legions and defeating Germanic tribes in a series of brutal campaigns. His popularity alarmed some in Rome, and his sudden death in Syria, possibly from poisoning, sparked suspicion and mourning across the empire.3

Gnaeus Julius Agricola (40–93 AD) – The Conqueror of Britain

Agricola, as governor of Britain, pushed Roman influence deep into the north, possibly reaching Scotland. He combined military campaigns with infrastructure building, roads, forts, and Romanised settlements, cementing imperial control.

His life, recorded by his son-in-law Tacitus, reflects both the ambition and restraint of a capable provincial commander.

Trajan (53–117 AD) – The Soldier Emperor

Known as the "Optimus Princeps" (Best Ruler), Trajan expanded the empire to its greatest extent, conquering Dacia and campaigning in Mesopotamia. A hands-on commander, he was equally respected for public works, such as bridges, harbours, and aqueducts, that improved Rome's prosperity

II. Philosophers and Thinkers – The Mind of Rome

Cicero (106–43 BC) – The Voice of the Republic

Marcus Tullius Cicero, a "new man" from outside Rome's aristocracy, rose to become consul and the republic's greatest orator. His speeches exposed the Catiline Conspiracy (an attempted coup d'état by Lucius Sergius Catilina (Catiline) to overthrow the Roman consuls of 63 BC) and his writings shaped Western ideas of law, citizenship, and duty. Cicero despised tyranny, opposing both Caesar and Mark Antony. His eloquence cost him his life: in 43 BC, Antony's soldiers killed him, and his severed head and hands were displayed in the Forum, a grim warning to others.

Seneca (c. 4 BC–65 AD) – The Stoic in the Palace

A Stoic philosopher and dramatist, Seneca tutored the young Nero, urging moderation and virtue. As a statesman, he helped govern in the early years of Nero's reign, but his philosophical ideals clashed with the emperor's excesses. Accused of conspiracy, Seneca was ordered to take his own life. His calm acceptance of death, recorded by Tacitus, embodied the Stoic principles he taught: that virtue matters more than life itself.

Marcus Aurelius (121–180 AD) – The Philosopher Emperor

The "philosopher emperor," Marcus Aurelius ruled during a time of almost constant warfare and plague. His Meditations, written in the field, are a window into the mind of a ruler who sought to live virtuously amid hardship. He saw power as a duty, not a privilege, and strove to embody Stoic ideals of endurance, justice, and humility.

Tacitus (c. 56–120 AD) - The Reluctant Historian of Power

A senator and historian, Tacitus chronicled Rome's emperors with a sharp, sometimes cynical eye. His Annals and Histories cover the Julio-Claudian dynasty and the Year of the Four Emperors, exposing the corrupting influence of absolute power. His concise, penetrating style remains one of the high points of Latin prose.

Tacitus

Suetonius (c. 69–122 AD) - The Chronicler of Emperors

Serving as imperial secretary under Hadrian, Suetonius had access to the imperial archives. His Lives of the Caesars offered vivid portraits of Rome's first twelve emperors, from the disciplined Augustus to the erratic Caligula, mixing official history with personal gossip. While sometimes scandalous, his work preserves invaluable detail about the lives and personalities of Rome's rulers.

Lucretius (c. 99–55 BC) – The Poet of Epicureanism

Author of De Rerum Natura (On the Nature of Things), Lucretius presented the Epicurean worldview, atoms, the nature of the soul, and the rejection of superstition, in sublime poetry. His work profoundly influenced later scientific and humanist thought.

Plotinus (204–270 AD) – The Mystic Philosopher

Founder of Neoplatonism, Plotinus sought to explain the soul's ascent to the divine "One." His teachings bridged classical philosophy and later Christian theology, shaping medieval and Renaissance thought.

III. Enemies Worthy of Rome – Shaping the Empire Through Opposition

Hannibal Barca (247–183 BC) – Rome's Greatest Foe

The Carthaginian general's crossing of the Alps with war elephants remains legendary. Hannibal inflicted crushing defeats at Trebia, Lake Trasimene, and Cannae, but ultimately was outmanoeuvred by Scipio Africanus. His campaigns forced Rome to rethink its military strategies.

Cleopatra VII (69–30 BC) – The Queen Who Defied Rome

The last Pharaoh of Egypt, Cleopatra allied herself with Julius Caesar and later Mark Antony in attempts to preserve Egypt's independence. Her defeat at Actium and suicide marked the end of the Ptolemaic kingdom and the rise of Roman Egypt.

Vercingetorix (82–46 BC) – The Gaul Who United the Tribes

Leader of the Gallic resistance against Caesar, Vercingetorix scored a notable victory at Gergovia before being trapped at Alesia. His courage and tactical skill made him a national hero in later French history.

Statue of Vercingetorix, Alesia, Côte-d'Or, France

Arminius (18 BC–21 AD) – The Destroyer of Legions

A Germanic chieftain trained as a Roman auxiliary, Arminius ambushed and annihilated three Roman legions in the Teutoburg Forest (9 CE), halting Roman expansion east of the Rhine.

Mithridates VI of Pontus (135–63 BC) – The Poison King

A formidable opponent in the East, Mithridates fought three wars against Rome, using both battlefield skill and propaganda to rally resistance across Asia Minor.

Arminius (c. 18 BC–19 AD) - The Liberator of Germania

Raised as a Roman auxiliary officer, Arminius knew Rome's tactics intimately. In 9 CE, he lured three legions into the Teutoburg Forest, where Germanic warriors annihilated them, a disaster that halted Rome's expansion east of the Rhine.

Though later betrayed and killed by his own people, Arminius became a German national hero centuries later.

IV. Greatness and Resistance in Perspective

Rome's story is a dialogue between ambition and opposition. Its greatest generals expanded its borders and secured its power, while philosophers and historians defined what it meant to be Roman. At the same time, its enemies, from Hannibal to Boudica, tested its limits, forcing it to adapt.

Together, these figures show that Rome's history is not just about legions and emperors, but about the human will, to build, to resist, to lead, and sometimes to defy fate itself.

CHAPTER 8. ROMAN SCIENCE, TECHNOLOGY, AND THE ECONOMY

The story of Rome is not just one of conquest and emperors, but also of builders, engineers, physicians, and merchants.

Though they were not scientists in the modern sense, the Romans inherited the intellectual traditions of the Greeks, Egyptians, and other ancient cultures, then turned them into tools to serve the needs of an empire that stretched from the wild hills of Scotland to the deserts of Arabia.

Their genius lay in application: harnessing knowledge to build roads that lasted for centuries, aqueducts that still stand, harbours that sheltered fleets, and farming systems that fed millions.

At its height, the Roman economy was the most sophisticated the ancient world had ever seen.

It bound together 60–70 million people in a vast network of cities, provinces, and trade routes, all underpinned by science and technology that were advanced for their time.

I. Roman Science – Borrowed Brilliance, Practical Purpose

The Romans were pragmatic. They rarely pursued theoretical science for its own sake, preferring to apply it in medicine, architecture, surveying, agriculture, and timekeeping. They drew heavily from Greek, Egyptian, Babylonian, and even Chinese knowledge, importing ideas and reshaping them to suit imperial needs.

1. Astronomy – The Sky as a Calendar

For Rome, astronomy was not about abstract theories of planetary motion, it was about measuring time and planning action.

The calendar governed harvests, tax collection, religious festivals, and military campaigns. Early Roman calendars were crude, but contact with Greek astronomers improved them.

The most lasting reform came from Julius Caesar in 45 BC: the Julian calendar, devised with the help of the Alexandrian astronomer Sosigenes. It introduced the leap year and brought Rome's year into near alignment with the solar year.

Astronomy also aided navigation. Sailors relied on star positions, especially constellations like Ursa Major and Orion, to guide them on the Mediterranean. While Ptolemy's complex models of planetary motion were studied by scholars, it was this practical sky-watching that mattered most to the empire.

2. Medicine – Healing in an Age of War

Roman medicine was an amalgamation of Greek theory and Roman pragmatism. The writings of Hippocrates and Galen underpinned elite medical practice, emphasising the balance of the four humours: blood, phlegm, black bile, and yellow bile.

But in army camps and bustling cities, medicine was practical and often improvisational.

Military surgeons set broken bones, stitched wounds, and amputated limbs with surprising skill, using bronze or iron scalpels, forceps, and cautery irons. Urban health benefited from aqueducts, sewers, and public baths, an unparalleled investment in public hygiene in the ancient world.

Roman doctors also pioneered aspects of public medicine: in major cities, there were medici paid by the state to treat the poor, while military medics served in legionary hospitals (valetudinaria). Herbal remedies, many imported from the provinces, were widely used, opium from Asia Minor, silphium from North Africa, and wine-infused antiseptics.

II. Roman Technology – Building for Eternity

If Greek science provided the theory, Roman technology provided the execution.

The empire's engineers worked with stone, brick, concrete, metal, and water to create an infrastructure so durable that parts of it are still in use.

1. Roads – The Imperial Arteries

Rome's road network stretched over 400,000 km, with more than 80,000 km paved in stone.

The layered construction of stone foundation, gravel bedding, fitted paving slabs, ensured strength and drainage. They allowed armies to move rapidly, tax collectors to reach the provinces, merchants to deliver goods, and messengers to carry orders across the empire.

2. Aqueducts – Water on Command

Aqueducts were Rome's most celebrated engineering triumph, enabling large cities to grow. They carried clean water from distant springs to cities, using carefully calculated gradients that relied purely on gravity. Some, like the Aqua Claudia and Aqua Marcia, ran for over 90 km. This water fed fountains, baths, sewers, and private homes, transforming urban life and public health.

The Roman aqueduct of Pont du Gard, France

▫▫DID YOU KNOW

- *The Trevi Fountain is supplied by an Ancient Aqueduct. The Aqua Vergine was constructed in 19 BC over 2000 years ago. Fifteen kilometres of it still survive today.*

Trevi fountain, Rome

- *Rome itself was served by 11 aqueducts by the end of the third century, with nearly 800 km of artificial water courses in total. Constructing these systems that used gravity to move water over long distances down tiny inclines was an astounding feat.*

- *Roman sewers are less celebrated but just as vital to urban life. The Cloaca Maxima was built from earlier open drains and canals, surviving through the entire Republic and Empire. Parts of it are still used as a drain today.*

3. Concrete – The Roman Secret Weapon

Opus caementicium, Roman concrete, revolutionised architecture. Strong, quick-setting, and versatile, it allowed the construction of domes, vaults, and vast public buildings.

The Pantheon's dome, still the largest unreinforced concrete dome in the world, shows just how advanced their materials science was.

Interior of the Roman Pantheon. Rome, Italy

4. Watermills – Harnessing Nature's Power

The Romans were among the first to use waterpower on an industrial scale. The Barbegal mills in southern Gaul, built in the 2nd century AD, comprised 16 waterwheels arranged in a cascading system, producing flour for an entire city. Watermills freed urban centres from sole dependence on hand grinding, hinting at the possibility of mechanised industry, though Rome never made that leap fully.

5. Steam Engines – A Glimpse of the Future

Roman inventors even experimented with steam power. In Alexandria, Hero of Alexandria described the aeolipile, a small device in which steam escaped from bent tubes, causing a sphere to spin. It was essentially the first recorded steam engine, but it was treated as a curiosity, not a source of power. In an empire reliant on cheap slave labour, there was little incentive to mechanise.

6. Military Engineering

The army's engineers could throw up marching camps, bridges, and siege works at astonishing speed. Julius Caesar's campaigns are full of examples: the Rhine bridge (55 BC), built in just ten days, intimidated Germanic tribes and demonstrated Roman reach.

▫▫DID YOU KNOW

- *Roman bridges still stand and are in use today. The Alcántara Bridge over the Tagus River in Spain is one of the most beautiful. It was completed in 106 AD under Emperor Trajan. 'I have built a bridge which will last forever,' reads an original inscription on the bridge.*

The Alcántara Bridge over the Tagus River in Spain

7. Ports and Harbours

Artificial harbours like Portus used massive concrete breakwaters to shelter fleets. These facilitated grain imports from Egypt and Africa, ensuring Rome's food security.

III. Roman Shipping and Navigation

The Roman economy was integrated through a network of roads, rivers, and sea routes. The Mediterranean was effectively a Roman lake (Mare Nostrum), enabling safe passage for merchant ships under the protection of the navy. Grain from Egypt, wine from Gaul, olive oil from Spain, and luxuries from India and China all travelled by sea.

1. Merchant Fleets

Roman merchant ships were broad-bellied and capable of carrying up to 400 tonnes of cargo.

Some were specialised: navis frumentariae carried grain, while amphora-laden vessels transported wine and oil.

2. Navigation Skills

Sailors preferred coastal routes, using landmarks and the sun for orientation, but in open water, they relied on stars. Seasonal winds, especially the summer etesian winds in the eastern Mediterranean, determined sailing schedules. Ports like Ostia and Portus near Rome were engineering marvels with breakwaters, lighthouses, and warehouses.

IV. Farming – Feeding the Empire

Agriculture was the foundation of the Roman economy, employing the vast majority of people.

1. *Latifundia and Villas*

Large estates (latifundia), often worked by slaves, dominated export agriculture.

They produced grain, wine, and olive oil for shipment across the empire. In contrast, smaller family farms produced food for local consumption.

2. *Farming Techniques*

Romans rotated crops, used manure as fertiliser, and irrigated fields where possible. Tools included iron ploughshares, sickles, and scythes. Viticulture and olive cultivation were especially profitable in Italy, Gaul, and Spain.

3. *Agricultural Science*

Writers like Columella and Varro recorded detailed instructions on planting, harvesting, and animal husbandry. Their treatises reveal a sophisticated understanding of soil management, grafting, and selective breeding.

V. The Roman Economy – A Web of Trade

The economy was a complex, interconnected system spanning three continents.

1. *Core Resources*

- From the West: Spanish silver, British tin and lead, Gallic wine.
- From the East: Egyptian grain, Arabian incense, Syrian glass, Indian spices, Chinese silk.

2. *Currency and Banking*

Standardised coinage - gold aureus, silver denarius, bronze sestertius - enabled stable trade.

Bankers (argentarii) managed deposits, loans, and currency exchange, especially in bustling ports.

3. Manufacturing

Rome had a vibrant manufacturing base:

- Pottery: Terra sigillata tableware was mass-produced and exported.

- Glass: Blown glassware from Syria was prized across the empire.

- Metalwork: Weapons, tools, and luxury silverware were produced in workshops from Gaul to Egypt.

VI. The Limits and Legacy of Roman Science and Technology

Why did Rome, with its ingenuity, never undergo an industrial revolution? The answer lies partly in economics: abundant slave labour reduced the incentive for mechanisation. Culturally, elites valued land ownership more than risky industrial investment.

Yet Rome's achievements endured. Their concrete inspired modern building; their road and aqueduct networks became the foundations of medieval Europe; their medical treatises guided physicians for over a thousand years; their shipping routes prefigured global trade networks.

Builders of a Practical Genius

The Romans did not seek to unlock the secrets of the universe, but to bend the natural world to human use. Astronomy gave them calendars to sow and reap, to sail and fight. Watermills, aqueducts, and concrete gave them the infrastructure to support vast cities. Medicine kept their armies in the field and their citizens healthy. Shipping and navigation bound the provinces together in one of the first truly globalised economies.

The Roman genius was not in dreaming of what might be, but in perfecting what could be done now, laying down stone by stone, arch by arch, ship by ship, the enduring framework of an empire.

PART III: DAILY LIFE IN THE ROMAN EMPIRE

CHAPTER 9: LIFE IN THE CITY AND COUNTRYSIDE

The Roman Empire was vast and diverse, spanning across many cultures, climates, and landscapes. Yet, despite these differences, the daily lives of those within the empire were shaped by shared customs, infrastructure, and social hierarchies. Whether in the bustling cities or in the quieter countryside, the Roman world was one of both luxury and hardship, innovation and tradition. This chapter delves into the daily life of Romans, exploring how they lived, worked, and interacted within the empire, as well as the physical and social environments that shaped their existence.

The Roman City: Forums, Aqueducts, Baths, Amphitheatres

Roman cities were carefully planned, designed to accommodate the needs of an empire that valued order, control, and spectacle. Cities were often built around a central forum, a public square that served as the heart of civic, political, and social life. It was here that citizens gathered to conduct business, make speeches, attend legal proceedings, or simply meet with friends. The forum also housed important buildings such as the Senate House (Curia), temples dedicated to various gods, and, occasionally, the basilica, which served as a meeting place for legal proceedings.

Perhaps the most iconic feature of Roman urban planning was the aqueducts, monumental engineering feats that supplied cities with fresh water. The Romans were masters of hydraulic engineering, and their aqueducts, often built from stone or brick, stretched across vast distances to bring water into cities for drinking, bathing, and irrigation. In cities like Rome, where the population often reached over a million, aqueducts were essential in ensuring a steady water supply.

Romans were famous for their public baths, which were not merely places for hygiene but also centers for socializing and relaxation. The thermae, or public baths, were often vast complexes that included not just hot and cold pools, but also exercise areas, gardens, and even libraries or lecture halls. Bathing was a daily ritual for many Romans, and it served as a communal activity, bringing people of different classes together in an environment of leisure and discussion.

Roman Baths in Bath Spa, England

Another hallmark of Roman cities was the amphitheatre. These large, open-air venues were used for public entertainment, including gladiatorial games, animal hunts, and mock naval battles. The Colosseum in Rome is the most famous example, but similar structures existed throughout the empire. These events, often violent and brutal, were both a form of entertainment and a means of demonstrating Roman power and dominance. They were a reflection of Rome's penchant for spectacle, as well as its control over life and death.

ᴅᴅDID YOU KNOW

- *The ancient Romans had a stadium for naval battles! Naumachia were spectacles with full-size ships that re-enacted famous sea battles. The first naumachia in Rome was hosted by Julius Caesar in 46 AD to celebrate his quadruple triumph. Later, Augustus would build the stagnum, a permanent stadium filled with water in the modern-day neighbourhood of Trastevere. These legendary Sea Battles were the most costly of all the games and were only held occasionally.*

Roman cities were not just centers of culture and entertainment; they were also places of commerce and innovation. Markets bustled with activity, selling everything from food to luxury goods, and craftsmen produced a wide variety of products, from pottery to weapons. The presence of shops and restaurants indicates the social importance of dining out, with both the rich and the poor partaking in meals in public spaces.

Daily Routines of Different Classes: Elites, Merchants, and Slaves

The Roman Empire was a highly stratified society, and daily life varied greatly depending on one's social standing. The elites, or patricians, enjoyed luxurious lifestyles, while the lower classes, including plebeians, merchants, and slaves, lived more modestly or endured hardship.

The Elites

For the wealthy elite, life was one of relative comfort and leisure. Roman elites typically lived in domus, large, elegant townhouses in the heart of the city. These homes featured grand atria, decorated with frescoes, mosaics, and sculptures, and gardens with fountains and greenery. Their diet consisted of fine food, including imported delicacies like oysters and wine from across the empire, and they enjoyed a social life centered around banquets and public events such as gladiatorial games or chariot races.

The daily routine for Roman elites was often dictated by public duties. Patricians might spend their mornings in the forum, participating in debates, legal cases, or political meetings. They would then retire to their homes for leisurely meals or to entertain guests. Their afternoons were often filled with exercise, hunting, attending the baths, or exercising in private palaestrae (gyms). Evenings could be spent at lavish feasts, which often lasted for hours and featured music, entertainment, and intellectual discussions.

ooDID YOU KNOW

- *The Romans had underfloor heating. It wasn't quite central heating as we know it today, but was based on the same idea. Hot air was heated by a furnace and distributed underneath the floor by terracotta pipes. This was called a hypocaust system and the same principle was also used for the Baths. On the Palatine Hill in Domitian's Palace pieces of the hypocaust can still be seen underneath a coloured marble floor.*

Merchants and Tradesmen

The merchants and artisans of Rome, while not as wealthy as the elite, also enjoyed a certain level of prosperity, particularly in cities with bustling markets. Merchants worked long hours, selling their goods in the fora or specialized markets, often traveling long distances to procure items for trade. These individuals had a varied diet, depending on their income, but they likely had access to more affordable foods such as bread, vegetables, and meats from local sources.

Artisans, including builders, metalworkers, and potters, lived and worked in cities but often in more modest conditions than their wealthier counterparts. These individuals lived in apartments above their workshops, and their daily lives were centered on their trades. They would work long hours in their workshops, creating everything from pottery to intricate jewelry.

Slaves

Perhaps the most marginalized group in Roman society were the slaves, who made up a large portion of the population. Slaves in Rome came from various backgrounds, often as prisoners of war, captured in raids, or born into slavery. They were typically employed in domestic service, agriculture, or large estates (latifundia). In urban areas, slaves could work as household servants, cooks, teachers, or even as accountants or physicians, depending on their skills.

Slaves did not have personal freedom and were subject to the whims of their masters. However, some could achieve a certain level of autonomy and even buy their freedom, becoming freedmen. Despite their lack of status, many slaves played an integral role in the daily functioning of the Roman economy and society.

Rural Life and Villa Economies

While the cities of Rome were centers of power, commerce, and culture, much of the empire's wealth came from its rural lands. Rural life revolved around agriculture, and the Roman economy was heavily dependent on the labor of peasants and slaves working large agricultural estates. These estates, known as latifundia, were owned by wealthy Romans or the state and were typically worked by slaves.

Life on the villa was hard and demanding. The primary crops were grains (such as wheat and barley), olives, and grapes, with livestock such as cattle, sheep, and pigs providing meat, milk, and wool. Many rural estates also produced luxury goods like wine and olive oil, which were exported throughout the empire.

In contrast to the bustling urban centers, life on rural estates was more isolated. The master of the villa was typically an absentee landowner, while a manager (or vilicus) oversaw the day-to-day operations of the estate. The peasants and slaves worked from dawn to dusk, performing back-breaking labor in the fields or caring for livestock. These workers had few rights, and their lives were dominated by the agricultural cycle.

Diet, Clothing, Sanitation, and Health

The daily lives of Romans were also shaped by practical concerns such as diet, clothing, sanitation, and health.

Diet: Roman cuisine was based on grains, vegetables, and legumes, but it varied depending on wealth and social class. The elite had access to a variety of meats (such as lamb, pork, and beef) and imported goods like fish and oysters. For the poorer classes, bread was the staple food, often accompanied by simple vegetables, fruits, and porridge. Wealthy Romans also enjoyed a wide variety of sweets, such as honey cakes and fruit preserves. They drank wine in large quantities, often diluted with water, and garum (a fermented fish sauce) was a common condiment.

▫▫DID YOU KNOW

- *Roman ate unusual foods…besides flamingo tongues, they also ate dormice, parrots, and ostrich brains!*

- *The Romans had a version of fast food, with vendors selling ready-to-eat meals. Most of the population lived in overcrowded accommodation without cooking facilities. Unlike today, it was the lowest level of society that ate out the most. There were numerous take-outs in ancient Rome like the thermopolia, snack bars where you could buy hot takeaway street food, and middle-class wine bars known as popina.*

- *There's a huge artificial hill in Rome called "Monte Testaccio" which is the result of the Romans dumping hundreds of thousands of used oil jars over the centuries as they could not reuse them due to the residue. The hill is still accessible today and it's literally a huge pile of thousands of layers of terracotta!*

Clothing: Roman clothing was primarily made from wool and linen, and the wealthy could afford fine garments adorned with intricate designs. Roman citizens typically wore the tunic, a simple garment that reached to the knees. The wealthy elite would wear a toga, a symbol of Roman citizenship. Women wore stolae, long dresses, and cloaks. Footwear varied from sandals to boots, depending on the wearer's class and occupation.

▢▢DID YOU KNOW

- *Purple dye was extremely expensive and rare, so only emperors and certain officials were allowed to wear it.*

Sanitation: Sanitation in Roman cities was surprisingly advanced. Public latrines were a common feature, and many Roman homes, especially those of the wealthy, had their own private bathrooms. The Romans built elaborate systems of underground drains and sewers, the most famous being the Cloaca Maxima in Rome, which drained the city's waste into the Tiber River. However, not all Roman citizens had access to these amenities, and sanitation could be poor in lower-class neighborhoods.

▢▢DID YOU KNOW

- *Ancient Romans used a communal sponge on a stick instead of toilet paper!*

- *The Romans sometimes used powdered mouse brains as toothpaste!*

- *Urine was a valuable commodity. Thanks to its ammonia content, it was sold as a chemical used in laundry and tanning leather. Outside of Rome itself fullones (Roman dry cleaners) would visit the toilets and collect the urine themselves. Urine became such a big business that Emperor Vespasian (69-79 AD) began taxing it. When his son, Titus, complained of the disgusting way his father was making money, Vespasian told his son to smell a gold coin. He then asked him if it stank, and when his son replied in the negative the Emperor replied "Yet it comes from urine."*

Health: The Romans had a relatively sophisticated understanding of medicine. Doctors treated illnesses using a variety of herbs, diets, and physical treatments like bathing. Surgery, though crude by modern standards, was practiced, and Roman military surgeons were known for their skills in treating wounds. Public baths also played a vital role in promoting personal hygiene and health, and

Romans believed in the therapeutic benefits of hot and cold water treatments. However, disease and poor sanitation were constant challenges, and epidemics, such as the plague of Cyprian in the 3rd century AD, would periodically ravage the empire.

ᴅᴅDID YOU KNOW

- *The Romans were the cleanest civilisation in their day. Romans realised keeping yourself clean relates to good health. They were the inventors of the modern Spa - Sana Per Acquam (Health through water) - and took their baths seriously.*

- *The Romans died from bad air. Malaria, which literally means "bad" (mal) "air" (aria) was rife in Rome in ancient times and was the biggest killer up until the 20th Century. The ancients knew that September and October brought the deadliest bouts, but didn't know this was due to the mosquitoes that thrived in these humid conditions.*

A Complex and Diverse World

Life in the Roman Empire was shaped by social hierarchy, cultural norms, and a complex system of infrastructure. From the bustling, vibrant cities with their aqueducts, baths, and forums to the rural villas and farms that provided the empire's wealth, Roman life was as diverse as the empire itself. Whether in the urban centers or on the farms, the Roman people were linked by their participation in the larger imperial system, one that defined their daily lives, their values, and their identities.

In the next chapter, we will turn our attention to Roman society, examining the roles of family, religion, and class, as well as the cultural aspects that permeated daily life in the empire.

CHAPTER 10: FAMILY, RELIGION, AND SOCIETY

The Roman Empire was a complex society built on a foundation of family, religion, and social customs. These aspects were not just personal; they were inextricably tied to the state, political life, and the Roman identity itself. The Romans placed great importance on the structure of the family, the rituals of their religion, and the entertainment that united the people, from the plebeians to the aristocracy. This chapter will explore the key elements that shaped Roman social life and how they affected the empire's culture, power, and identity.

The Roman Family: Paterfamilias, Marriage, and Roles of Women

At the heart of Roman society was the family, or familia, which was not just a unit of biological relations but a broader social structure governed by strict rules. The head of the family was the paterfamilias, the eldest male, who held absolute power over all members of the household, including his wife, children, and slaves. The paterfamilias controlled the family's property, had the authority to arrange marriages, and even exercised the right of life and death over family members in certain cases, although this was a power seldom used.

Marriage in Rome was an institution designed to strengthen social and political alliances, and it played a crucial role in maintaining the social order. Patricians and plebeians alike arranged marriages to further their wealth and influence. Marriages were typically arranged by the fathers of the bride and groom, and while love could certainly develop over time, the primary purpose of marriage was to produce legitimate heirs. The bride's family would typically provide a dowry, and the groom's family would arrange a proper home and livelihood for his new wife.

The role of women in Roman society was complex. Women were considered the caretakers of the home, tasked with running the household, bearing children, and managing the family's domestic affairs. However, women could also hold significant influence in Roman society, especially in wealthier families. Some women, like Livia Drusilla (the wife of Emperor Augustus) and Agrippina the

Younger (mother of Emperor Nero), wielded considerable political power behind the scenes, even if they were not allowed to hold official political office themselves.

While women in Roman society were often subject to the control of male relatives, they were also revered as the preservers of Roman values and morality. The ideal Roman woman was modest, loyal, and devoted to her family, epitomized by the figure of Cornelia, the mother of the Gracchi brothers, who symbolized the virtues of Roman motherhood.

Roman Religion: Gods, Myths, and the Sacred Life of Rome

Roman civilization was built on stone, iron, and law, but also on the unseen foundations of faith, ritual, and the gods. From the smoky altars of the Forum to the rural shrines at crossroads, from whispered prayers in soldiers' tents to the vast, incense-filled temples of Jupiter and Venus, religion in Rome was not a private matter. It was the glue that bound the community together, the moral compass of the state, and, in times of war, the rallying cry of legions.

Religion was less about personal salvation and more about maintaining the correct forms, the right words, the right gestures, at the right time.

Yet Roman religion was never static. It was a living, evolving tapestry woven from native Italic traditions, myths borrowed from Greece - Jupiter hurling thunderbolts, Venus rising from the sea - foreign cults, imperial worship, and, eventually, the spread of Christianity. To understand Rome's soul, one must understand its gods.

The Origins: From Village Spirits to the Capitoline Triad

The earliest Romans lived in an animistic world. Every field, spring, and hearth was thought to have its spirit, the numina, invisible forces that required respect through proper ritual. The household gods (Lares and Penates) guarded the family's welfare, while Vesta, goddess of the hearth, symbolized the fire of the state itself.

Over time, as Rome grew from a cluster of huts into a kingdom and then a republic, these local deities were elevated into a formal pantheon. The most important gods resided on the Capitoline Hill in a magnificent temple dedicated to the Capitoline Triad:

- Jupiter Optimus Maximus – King of the gods, wielder of the thunderbolt, protector of the Roman state.
- Juno – Queen of the gods, guardian of women and marriage.
- Minerva – Goddess of wisdom, war strategy, and crafts.

Every triumph, every declaration of war, every peace treaty was ratified under the watchful gaze of these gods.

Borrowed Glory: The Greek Influence

By the 3rd century BC, Roman religion had been deeply enriched by contact with the Greek world. The Romans identified their gods with the Greek pantheon - Jupiter with Zeus, Mars with Ares, Venus with Aphrodite - and imported their myths wholesale, often giving them a Roman twist.

Epic tales of Hercules' labors, the wanderings of Odysseus, or the loves of the gods became part of Roman cultural life. But the Romans were less interested in the purely poetic aspects of Greek mythology than in its moral and political use. Myths served as moral lessons, symbols of divine favor, and even political propaganda. The poet Virgil famously linked Rome's origins to the Trojan hero Aeneas in The Aeneid, making the city's birth part of a grand divine plan.

Other Gods included:

- Mars – Once a god of agriculture, Mars became the Roman god of war, father of Romulus and Remus.
- Venus – Goddess of love, beauty, and fertility; claimed as an ancestor by Julius Caesar's family.

- Mercury – God of commerce, travel, and messages.

- Neptune – God of the sea, worshipped especially by sailors.

- Diana – Goddess of the hunt and the moon.

- Vulcan – God of fire and metalwork.

- Apollo – Imported wholesale from Greece, god of the sun, prophecy, and music.

- Saturn – An ancient agricultural god, honoured in the wild and joyful festival of Saturnalia.

Ritual and Priesthood: The Machinery of Faith

Religion in Rome was formal, public, and ritualistic. The gods were not approached casually; they demanded precise offerings, correct prayers, and appropriate festivals. Mistakes in ceremony could nullify the ritual, requiring it to be repeated — a principle called vitium.

The religious system was maintained by a complex priesthood:

- Pontifex Maximus – The chief priest of Rome, responsible for overseeing religious law.

- Augurs – Interpreters of the will of the gods through signs such as the flight of birds.

- Vestal Virgins – Priestesses of Vesta, charged with keeping the sacred flame burning in the Forum. Their chastity was considered essential to the security of Rome.

- Flamines – Priests devoted to specific gods, such as Jupiter, Mars, or Quirinus.

Religious festivals such as Lupercalia, Saturnalia, Parilia, and many more, punctuated the year, binding the community in a shared cycle of sacred time.

Foreign Cults and Mystery Religions

Rome's tolerance for foreign gods was extraordinary. As the empire expanded, it adopted deities from conquered peoples. These included:

The Great Mother (Magna Mater) from Phrygia

- Isis from Egypt, goddess of motherhood and magic.

- Mithras from Persia, a god of soldiers, worshipped in underground temples (mithraea).

- Cybele, the Great Mother, from Anatolia, whose ecstatic rites shocked traditional Romans.

- Serapis, a Greco-Egyptian fusion deity.

Some of these religions, especially the so-called mystery cults, offered personal salvation and an afterlife, ideas absent from traditional Roman religion. Initiates of the Mithraic mysteries met in underground temples and participated in secret rites. The cult of Isis promised rebirth and protection, appealing to soldiers, merchants, and women alike.

The Rise of Imperial Cult

From Augustus onward, the emperors were not only political leaders but also divine figures, or at least divinely favored. In the provinces, temples were dedicated to "Rome and the Emperor," blending loyalty to the state with worship of the ruler. In the East, where the idea of god-kings was older, emperors like Hadrian and Trajan were openly venerated as living gods.

The imperial cult reinforced unity across a diverse empire. To refuse participation, as early Christians often did, was seen as an act of political rebellion.

Philosophy and Religion

For Rome's educated elite, Greek philosophy offered new ways to understand the divine. Stoicism, embraced by figures like Seneca and Emperor Marcus Aurelius, taught that the universe was governed by reason (logos) and that virtue was the highest good. Epicureanism, represented by the poet Lucretius, rejected fear of the gods and death, advocating a life of moderation.

These philosophies did not replace traditional worship but often coexisted with it, shaping personal beliefs and moral conduct.

Myths of Rome's Foundation

No account of Roman religion is complete without its origin legends, which were themselves sacred narratives.

Romulus and Remus, twin sons of Mars, abandoned at birth, suckled by a she-wolf, and destined to found Rome. In the myth, Romulus kills Remus in a dispute over the city's location, becoming the first king.

Romulus and Remus, Louvre Museum, France

Aeneas, the Trojan hero who, guided by the gods, carried his father from burning Troy and journeyed to Italy. His descendants were said to be Rome's founders.

These myths were more than stories, they were political statements, affirming Rome's divine destiny.

From Tolerance to Conflict: Christianity and Rome

The earliest Christians in Rome were a small, often persecuted minority. Their refusal to worship the emperor or participate in public sacrifices made them targets for suspicion. Persecutions under emperors like Nero and Diocletian were brutal but sporadic.

Yet the appeal of Christianity with its promise of eternal life, its sense of community, and its moral clarity, spread across all classes. In 313 AD, Constantine the Great issued the Edict of Milan, granting freedom of worship. By the end of the 4th century, under Theodosius I, Christianity became the official religion of the empire, and the old pagan temples began to fall silent.

⌑⌑DID YOU KNOW

- *The Battle of the Milvian Bridge in 312 AD is important for its role in the advance of Christianity. Two emperors, Constantine and Maxentius, were battling for power. Chronicles recount Constantine receiving a vision from the Christian god, offering victory if his men decorated their shields with Christian symbols. Whether true or not, the battle confirmed Constantine as sole ruler of the Western Roman Empire and a year later Christianity was legally recognised and tolerated by Rome.*

Astronomy, Omens, and Astrology

While Roman religion was deeply ritualistic, it also intersected with what we would now call science. Astronomical observation played a key role in setting festival dates and interpreting omens. Eclipses, comets, and unusual celestial events were considered messages from the gods.

Astrology, imported from the Hellenistic world, became a passion for many Romans, from common citizens to emperors like Tiberius. Horoscopes and planetary alignments were thought to reveal destiny itself.

Sacred Spaces: Temples, Shrines, and Altars

Temples were the architectural heart of Roman religion. They were not places for congregational worship but the dwelling places of the gods' images. The most famous, the Pantheon in Rome, was dedicated to "all gods" and remains one of the most remarkable buildings of antiquity.

In rural areas, simple roadside shrines honored local spirits. Every Roman army camp had its sacellum (sacred enclosure), and every home its lararium, a small altar to the household gods.

Festivals and Public Games

Religion and entertainment were deeply intertwined. Public games (ludi) in honor of the gods could involve chariot races, theatrical performances, or gladiatorial combats. The Colosseum itself was often the stage for religiously sanctioned spectacles.

Festivals like Saturnalia — a midwinter celebration in honor of Saturn — temporarily overturned social order, with slaves feasting as equals to masters. It was a season of gift-giving, merriment, and even mild anarchy, and its customs would echo in later European holiday traditions.

Other festivals included:

- Lupercalia (February) – A fertility festival involving goat sacrifices and ritual running through the streets.
- Parilia – A festival for the founding of Rome.
- Ludi Romani – Games in honour of Jupiter, featuring chariot races and theatrical performances.

The End of the Old Gods

By the late empire, the temples of Jupiter and Mars stood quiet, their altars cold. Statues of emperors were replaced by Christian crosses; pagan festivals were either suppressed or reinterpreted. But the old gods did not vanish entirely. Their myths were preserved in literature, their images in art, and their names in the planets we still chart in our skies: Mars, Venus, Jupiter, Saturn.

In truth, the Roman gods never fully died. They simply changed forms — living on in Renaissance paintings, Enlightenment philosophy, and even in modern popular culture.

The Gods' Long Shadow

Roman religion was not simply about belief, it was about identity, duty, and the cosmic order. It shaped law, art, politics, and daily life. Its adaptability allowed it to absorb and integrate the gods of Greece, Egypt, and beyond. Even in its decline, its imagery and myths seeded the foundations of Western civilization.

In the end, the Roman gods and their rituals gave way to a new faith, but their legacy is still with us, in our language, our architecture, our festivals, and the stories we tell about the origins of the world and ourselves.

Entertainment and Leisure: Gladiators, Theatre, Chariot Racing

For Romans, entertainment was an important part of life, and the empire's rulers used public spectacles as a means of both appeasing the masses and displaying Roman power and wealth. These spectacles were a central part of Roman identity and were designed to provide not only enjoyment but also to reinforce the values of Roman strength, discipline, and cultural pride.

Gladiatorial games were perhaps the most iconic form of Roman entertainment. Gladiators were typically slaves or prisoners of war who were trained to fight in the arena. These men fought to the death, either in combat with one another or with wild animals, in massive amphitheaters such as the Colosseum in Rome. The games were brutal and often deadly, but they served a vital social function: they were a means of displaying Roman military might, offering a form of spectacle that connected the people to the empire's conquests. Emperors would use the games to curry favor with the public, and wealthy elites often funded these events as a means of displaying their own status.

The Colosseum in Rome

Theatre was another popular form of entertainment, although it did not carry the same violent connotations as gladiatorial games. Roman theatre was influenced by Greek traditions and included comedies, tragedies, and farces. Performances were held in large open-air theatres, and actors and playwrights enjoyed a measure of fame and social recognition. Theatre provided an opportunity for Romans to reflect on their values, social issues, and the complexities of their own lives.

Chariot racing, held in the Circus Maximus and other large arenas, was another major form of entertainment. Chariot races were highly competitive, with teams of horses racing around a large track at high speeds. The races were immensely popular and attracted thousands of spectators. Like gladiatorial games, they were often used by emperors to entertain the public and to keep the plebeians content. The races were not only dangerous but also very political, as fans of different teams (often represented by colors) would develop strong rivalries, sometimes leading to violent riots.

The Tapestry of Roman Life

Roman society was multifaceted and dynamic, with a complex interplay between family structures, religious practices, and forms of entertainment. The Romans placed great importance on family and social roles, which were reflected in the legal and political structures of the state. Religion was a central pillar of Roman life, with a vast pantheon of gods and rituals permeating everyday existence. At the same time, mystery cults and astrology offered more personalized avenues for spiritual fulfillment, while the rise of Christianity would eventually reshape the entire empire.

The entertainment and leisure activities of the Romans, particularly gladiatorial games, theatre, and chariot racing, illustrated both the grandeur and brutality of Roman culture. These spectacles were not just forms of escapism; they were deeply tied to Roman values and were used to demonstrate the power and prestige of the empire. Together, these elements formed the fabric of Roman society, creating a world that was as diverse and complex as the empire itself.

In the next chapter, we will explore the institution of slavery in the Roman world, examining its prevalence, the roles of slaves, and the social dynamics of Roman servitude.

CHAPTER 11: BLOOD AND SAND – THE WORLD OF THE GLADIATOR

The Roar of the Arena

In the heart of Rome, the Colosseum rose like a giant of stone and mortar, its vast oval tiers filled with fifty thousand spectators. Senators, merchants, freedmen, slaves, and women of every station gathered together, united by one expectation: the promise of blood. For the Romans, few spectacles captured the spirit of their empire more than the gladiatorial games. They were displays of power and discipline, of violence harnessed for entertainment, and of Rome's mastery over life and death. To understand the gladiator is to glimpse both the brutality and the brilliance of Roman civilization.

Origins of the Gladiators

The gladiatorial tradition did not begin as entertainment. Its roots lay in the funerary rituals of early Italy, particularly among the Etruscans and Campanians. At the funeral of a noble, slaves or captives were made to fight to the death, their blood a sacrifice to honor the dead. By the third century BC, the Romans had adopted and formalized the practice.

The Gladiator by Nicolao Landucci

The first recorded Roman gladiatorial combat occurred in 264 BC, when three pairs fought in Rome as part of a funeral rite for a senator. Over the following centuries, the practice expanded beyond funerals, becoming public entertainment sponsored by ambitious politicians eager to curry favor with the people. By the late Republic, games were no longer pious rituals but carefully staged spectacles that shaped careers and commanded public loyalty.

Who Were the Gladiators?

Contrary to the popular image of gladiators as free men lured by glory, the majority were slaves, criminals, or prisoners of war.

- Slaves were often sold into the ludus (gladiator school) by their masters.
- Criminals convicted of capital crimes might be condemned ad ludum ("to the school") or ad gladium ("to the sword"), effectively sentenced

to fight until death.

- Prisoners of war filled the ranks after Rome's conquests - Gauls, Thracians, and later Dacians and Germans. Their ethnic identities often shaped their fighting styles in the arena.

Yet not all gladiators were coerced. Some were volunteers (auctorati). Driven by poverty, debt, or a desire for fame, these men bound themselves by oath to the gladiator's life, surrendering their legal and social status in return for the promise of pay, food, and the chance at glory. To the Romans, such men carried a peculiar shame, for a citizen to choose the arena was to embrace infamy, yet they were often admired for their courage.

Life in the Gladiator Schools

Gladiators lived in the ludi gladiatorii, specialized training schools overseen by a lanista, who was part coach, part slave-master. The most famous of these schools stood at Capua and later in Rome itself, near the Colosseum, where the Ludus Magnus housed hundreds of fighters.

Inside, gladiators lived under strict discipline. They trained daily, practicing strikes, parries, and footwork with wooden weapons weighted to build strength. Different classes of gladiators mastered different styles — the heavily armored secutor, the lightly armed retiarius with net and trident, the murmillo with his crested helmet, or the exotic Thraex with curved sword and small shield.

Gladiators from the Zliten mosaic.

Despite the harshness, conditions were not uniformly grim. Gladiators were valuable investments: owners fed them well, provided medical care, and ensured they were trained by professionals. Archaeological evidence from Pompeii shows a barracks with graffiti praising gladiators by name, suggesting they formed close bonds and even attracted admirers.

The Life of a Gladiator: Discipline, Honor, and Stigma

The gladiator's life was one of contradictions. On the one hand, he lived under the shadow of infamy, stripped of legal rights and condemned to a brutal existence. On the other, he could achieve a measure of fame, wealth, and admiration unknown to most slaves.

Spectators adored skilled fighters, showering them with gifts and chanting their names. Successful gladiators could even win freedom, symbolized by the rudis, a wooden sword awarded for exceptional valor or long service. Some became celebrities, their images painted on walls and vases, their exploits retold in taverns. Women were notorious for their fascination with gladiators: poets like Juvenal and Martial sneered at noble ladies who lusted after these men of the arena.

Yet society never let them forget their disgrace. Gladiators were admired, but never respected. They lived at the edge of honor, celebrated on the sands but excluded from true citizenship.

The Games: Ritual and Spectacle

A gladiatorial show, or munus, followed a well-established pattern. The day began with a procession into the arena: gladiators marched before the crowd, saluting the sponsor of the games and the emperor if present. The opening acts might include displays of exotic animals or executions of condemned criminals.

The main event was the paired combats. Gladiators were carefully matched — style against style, strength against agility. The fights were not chaotic melees but regulated contests, overseen by referees who could stop the combat if rules were broken.

Despite modern images of constant slaughter, gladiators did not always fight to the death. Training them was expensive, and organizers preferred repeated contests to maximize value. Still, death was always a possibility. When a gladiator was wounded and unable to continue, the decision of life or death rested with the sponsor, often guided by the crowd's reaction. A gesture of mercy or condemnation could seal a man's fate.

Arenas and Audiences

While the Colosseum in Rome is the most famous, amphitheaters dotted the empire, from Pompeii to Nîmes, from Carthage to Londinium. These stone ovals symbolized Rome's reach and power, bringing the spectacle of the games to provincial towns.

For the audience, the games were both entertainment and political theater. The poor enjoyed free admission; the elite showcased their wealth and generosity by sponsoring lavish spectacles. In the stands, social divisions were suspended: senators, equestrians, plebeians, and women all gathered under one roof, sharing in the raw thrill of combat.

Who Did Gladiators Fight?

Gladiators typically fought other gladiators, matched for contrast and spectacle. The lightly armed retiarius with net and trident faced the secutor with heavy shield and helmet designed to resist his attacks. The murmillo, with his broad shield and gladius, often clashed with the Thraex, whose curved sword and small shield demanded agility.

There were also special categories:

- Bestiarii fought wild beasts — lions, leopards, bears, and elephants imported at enormous expense.

- Venatores staged hunts in the arena, displaying skill and daring against dangerous animals.

- Occasionally, large-scale mock battles (naumachiae) were staged, sometimes even flooding arenas for simulated naval combat.

A Murmillo Gladiator Fights a Barbary Lion in the colosseum in Rome during a condemnation of beasts.

These contests blurred the line between sport and spectacle, blending martial discipline with theatrical display.

Treatment and Mortality

Life expectancy for a gladiator was short, though not always as brief as popular imagination suggests. Inscriptions suggest that many fought in a dozen or more contests before dying. Survival depended on skill, luck, and the favor of the crowd.

Medical evidence from gladiator cemeteries, such as that at Ephesus, reveals well-healed wounds and specialized care. Doctors attached to the schools developed surgical skills, and gladiators sometimes lived long enough to become trainers. Still, the ever-present risk of sudden death was part of their existence — and their allure.

Gladiators in Roman Culture and Imagination

To the Romans, the games embodied their values: discipline, courage, endurance in the face of death. Gladiators represented both the lowest of the low and the highest virtues of martial spirit. They were despised and admired in equal measure.

Philosophers like Seneca used gladiators as moral exemplars, citing their courage as a model for stoic endurance. At the same time, moralists condemned the bloodlust of the crowds and the debasement of human life. Even some emperors wavered: Augustus regulated the games, Marcus Aurelius is said to have disliked them, while Commodus notoriously fought as a gladiator himself.

The End of the Gladiatorial Games

The decline of gladiatorial combat came gradually. By the third century AD, the empire's financial and political crises made staging large-scale spectacles difficult. Christianity, spreading through the empire, also condemned the games as cruel and immoral. By the early fifth century, the gladiatorial contests had vanished, replaced by chariot racing and theatrical entertainments.

Yet the image of the gladiator endured, a potent symbol of Rome's grandeur and cruelty alike.

The Legacy of Blood and Sand

Gladiators were far more than men who fought in the arena. They embodied the contradictions of Rome itself: ruthless yet disciplined, savage yet spectacular, despised yet adored. Their lives, played out on the sands of amphitheaters, were both entertainment and ritual, binding Roman society in a shared experience of blood and spectacle.

Though centuries have passed since the last gladiator fell beneath the roar of the crowd, their memory lingers in our imagination, the flash of steel, the cry of the mob, and the eternal struggle between life and death beneath the Roman sun.

CHAPTER 12: SLAVERY AND CLASS IN THE ROMAN WORLD

Slavery was the backbone of Roman society, an institution so integral to its economy, daily life, and political structure that it often went unremarked upon in the historical record. From the fields of Italy to the villas of the aristocracy, from the mines of Spain to the imperial palaces, slaves were a vital part of Roman life. This chapter explores the prevalence of slavery, the roles and social mobility of slaves, the class structure of Roman society, and the tensions that arose from inequality and social reforms.

The Prevalence of Slavery: Sources and Roles

Slavery in Rome was not based on race or ethnicity, as it was in later historical periods. Instead, slavery was a status that one could fall into due to war, conquest, debt, or birth. Slaves were acquired through military conquest, as prisoners of war were often sold into slavery. The Romans were notorious for their expansionist ambitions, and their conquests across Europe, North Africa, and the Near East provided them with a steady supply of slaves. During the Punic Wars, for instance, thousands of captives from Carthage were brought back to Rome as slaves.

Another important source of slaves was the practice of child slavery, whereby children born to enslaved parents would automatically inherit their parents' status. Additionally, some individuals sold themselves into slavery as a means of paying off debts. While the circumstances varied, the result was always the same: the slave was considered the property of their owner, with no rights to personal freedom.

Slaves in Roman society served in a variety of roles, from agricultural laborers in the fields to highly skilled professionals in the city. In wealthy households, slaves acted as domestics -cooks, cleaners, tutors, and caretakers. They were often educated and trained in specific trades, such as blacksmithing, teaching, or medicine. In the imperial household, slaves held prestigious roles as secretaries, chamberlains, and personal attendants to the emperor.

While many slaves worked on large estates in rural Italy, others toiled in the mines or quarries, often enduring brutal conditions. Gladiators were also slaves, trained to fight in the arena for the entertainment of the masses. The life of a slave was harsh and offered few prospects for freedom, but the possibility of manumission, the act of being freed by one's owner, was a distant hope for some. In some cases, slaves could buy their freedom, or it could be granted as a reward for loyal service.

▫▫DID YOU KNOW

- *Spartacus (111 – 71 BC) was an escaped gladiator who led a slave revolt in 73 BC. His powerful forces threatened Rome during the Third Servile War. He was a Thracian (from southeast Europe, in modern-day Bulgaria, Romania and North Macedonia), but little is known about him beyond his military skill. The defeated slaves were crucified.*

Freedmen and Social Mobility

Although slavery was a fixed status in the Roman world, freedmen (former slaves who had been granted their freedom) represented an interesting anomaly in the rigid Roman class system. Roman slaves were protected by law and could actually buy their freedom. Unlike more recent forms of slavery, Roman slaves were paid a small amount of money and given board and lodgings. Over time if they could save enough money, they could buy their freedom. Many slaves were granted freedom by their masters for services well done. Freed slaves often went on to become successful businessmen with the help of their masters.

While freedmen did not enjoy the full legal status of a freeborn Roman citizen, they were still able to enjoy a considerable degree of social mobility, particularly if they amassed wealth or were successful in trade.

Freedmen could acquire property, enter into contracts, and marry Roman citizens. Some even became wealthy merchants or successful artisans. The most fortunate freedmen could rise to positions of influence, leveraging their wealth and connections to gain access to the upper echelons of Roman society. In fact, some emperors, such as Emperor Claudius, were themselves the descendants of freedmen, illustrating how social mobility, while limited, was still possible in the empire.

However, despite these opportunities, freedmen were still viewed with some disdain by the aristocratic classes. They were often looked down upon as socially inferior, even though their wealth and influence sometimes allowed them to challenge the power of the established patrician class. The term "freedman" itself carried an air of stigma, and their descendants, even if wealthy, could find themselves relegated to a lower social status.

Patricians, Plebeians, and the Equestrian Order

At the top of the Roman social hierarchy were the patricians, a hereditary aristocratic class that held political and social power. Patricians were the landowners, senators, and high-ranking officials in Roman society. They controlled most of the wealth and had exclusive access to key positions of power, such as the consulship, the highest elected office in the Roman Republic.

Below the patricians were the plebeians, the common people. They made up the bulk of the Roman population and worked as farmers, laborers, artisans, and soldiers. Initially, the plebeians had little political power, but over time they gained significant rights, particularly through the Conflict of the Orders, a long struggle between the patricians and plebeians that eventually led to the establishment of the Tribunate. The tribunes were plebeian officials with the power to veto legislation that they saw as harmful to the interests of the plebs.

Despite their numerical superiority, plebeians had limited opportunities for social mobility. Although a wealthy plebeian could eventually gain access to the political elite, the majority remained confined to the lower rungs of Roman society, working in manual labor and subsistence farming. However, over time, the distinction between patricians and plebeians became less rigid, especially as wealth and political influence began to play a larger role in defining social status.

One of the more fluid and dynamic classes within Roman society was the equestrian order (also known as the equites). This group consisted of wealthy individuals who were not quite patricians but who had sufficient wealth to be eligible to serve in the cavalry of the Roman army. The equites were often involved in business and trade and played an important role in financing the Roman state, especially during times of war. Over time, the equites became a powerful class, especially in the late Republic and the early Empire. They were heavily involved in administrative and financial affairs and, in some cases, even entered the Senate.

Social Tensions and Reforms: The Gracchi, Grain Dole, and the Struggles for Equality

Roman society was plagued by stark social inequalities. While the patricians and the equites enjoyed political and economic power, the plebeians often faced poverty, harsh living conditions, and little opportunity for advancement. Tensions between these classes frequently boiled over into social unrest, and several key reforms were introduced to address these disparities.

One of the most notable reform movements came from the Gracchi brothers, Tiberius Gracchus and Gaius Gracchus, who, in the late 2nd century BC, attempted to address the growing inequality between the rich and poor. Tiberius, as a tribune, introduced land reforms that aimed to redistribute public land to the plebeians, while his brother Gaius attempted to expand the grain dole (the state-sponsored distribution of free or subsidized grain) to alleviate the suffering of the lower classes.

Both brothers were met with fierce opposition from the Senate and the aristocracy, and their reform movements ultimately ended in tragedy. Tiberius was killed by a mob of senators, and Gaius died in a similar fashion, with his reforms failing to gain lasting traction. Despite their deaths, the Gracchi brothers' efforts signaled the growing awareness of the need for social and economic reforms in the Roman state.

The grain dole, or annona, was another significant social policy aimed at alleviating poverty among the plebeians. The state provided free or subsidized grain to Roman citizens, particularly those in the urban slums, ensuring that the lower classes had enough food to survive. Over time, this system became an important tool for maintaining political stability in Rome, as emperors and politicians would use the grain dole as a means of winning favor with the people. The annona was crucial in securing the loyalty of the plebeians, who made up a significant portion of the Roman electorate.

Despite these reforms, social inequality continued to persist throughout the Roman Republic and into the Empire. The gap between the rich and poor remained vast, and while some emperors, like Augustus and Trajan, attempted to address social issues, the class divisions within Roman society were never fully resolved. In the end, the rich and powerful continued to wield most of the political and economic power, while the majority of the population remained subject to the whims of the elite.

The Unyielding Hierarchy of Roman Society

The social structure of Rome was complex and deeply entrenched, built on the foundation of slavery, patronage, and hierarchy. Slaves, freedmen, and citizens lived in a rigid system of class divisions that defined their rights, opportunities, and obligations. While the Roman Empire offered some avenues for social mobility, particularly for freedmen, the social order was largely inflexible.

The patricians and plebeians, despite centuries of struggle and reform, continued to exist in a state of tension. Social unrest, particularly in the form of populist leaders like the Gracchi, highlighted the pressures of inequality that the Roman state could not fully resolve. Although some reforms were introduced, the fundamental class structures of Rome remained largely intact.

This rigid class system and its corresponding tensions played a significant role in the downfall of the Roman Republic and the transition to empire. By the time the empire reached its peak, social divisions had only intensified, contributing to the growing discontent among the lower classes and eventual political upheaval.

In the next chapter, we will examine the crisis and fall of the Western Roman Empire, focusing on the factors that led to its collapse, including internal corruption, external invasions, and the disintegration of the social and political fabric that had once held it together.

PART IV: DECLINE AND LEGACY

CHAPTER 13: CRISIS AND FALL OF THE WESTERN EMPIRE

The Roman Empire, once the epitome of strength and stability, found itself struggling to maintain its unity and power during the 3rd century AD. Over time, the cracks in the imperial structure grew too wide to ignore, leading to the eventual fragmentation and collapse of the Western Roman Empire. From internal strife and economic collapse to barbarian invasions and the rise of Christianity, the causes of Rome's decline were multifaceted and deeply intertwined.

This chapter will explore the crisis of the third century, the reforms of Diocletian and Constantine, the invasions that shattered the Empire, and the final fall of the Western Roman Empire.

The Third Century Crisis: Civil Wars and Economic Collapse

The 3rd century AD was a period of profound turmoil for the Roman Empire, known as the Crisis of the Third Century. It was marked by a combination of civil wars, political instability, economic decline, and external invasions. The Empire was beset on all sides, and its internal structure, which had once been the envy of the world, began to crumble under the pressure of these forces.

Civil Wars and Political Instability

The Crisis of the Third Century began with the assassination of Emperor Severus Alexander in 235 AD. His death triggered a period of instability, during which over twenty emperors came to power in rapid succession, many of whom were generals who seized power through force or manipulation. These rulers, known as the Barracks Emperors, were often more concerned with maintaining their hold on power than governing effectively.

During this chaotic period, Rome was split into several competing factions. The Empire was fragmented, with regions breaking away from central authority. This era also witnessed the rise of the Gallic Empire (260–274 AD), which encompassed the western provinces of Gaul, Britain, and Hispania, and the Palmyrene Empire (260–273 AD), which controlled the eastern provinces, including Syria, Egypt, and parts of Asia Minor. These breakaway empires further weakened the unity of the Roman state.

Economic Collapse

The constant warfare, coupled with inflation, heavy taxation, and the debasement of currency, led to severe economic decline. The monetary system was in disarray, as emperors reduced the silver content of coins to make more money, which in turn caused runaway inflation. The economy became increasingly reliant on barter rather than cash transactions. Trade suffered, as did agriculture, as war and instability disrupted agricultural production.

The population was also decimated by constant warfare and famine, further weakening the Empire's economic foundations. The infrastructure that had once supported the vast empire, roads, aqueducts, and public buildings, fell into disrepair, further compounding the sense of decline.

Diocletian's Reforms and the Tetrarchy

In the face of this widespread crisis, Emperor Diocletian (reigned 284–305 AD) emerged as the man who would try to restore order to the Empire. His reign marked a turning point in the history of Rome, as Diocletian implemented a series of radical reforms aimed at stabilizing the Empire and addressing the issues that had led to the crisis.

Emperor Diocletian

The Tetrarchy

One of Diocletian's most significant reforms was the establishment of the Tetrarchy (meaning "rule of four"). Recognizing the vastness and complexity of the Roman Empire, Diocletian divided the Empire into four administrative regions, each governed by a leader. He took the title of Augustus (the senior emperor) in the eastern part of the Empire and appointed Maximian as Augustus of the western part. They were each supported by a Caesar (junior emperor), Galerius in the east and Constantius in the west.

This division allowed for more localized and effective rule, with each emperor responsible for a smaller section of the Empire. The idea was that by splitting the responsibilities of governing and military command, the Empire could be defended more effectively, and leadership could be more focused. It also provided a clear line of succession, with the Caesars expected to eventually replace the Augusti when their terms ended.

While the Tetrarchy helped stabilize the Empire temporarily, it also sowed the seeds of future division. Following Diocletian's abdication in 305 AD, the system broke down as rivalry and power struggles ensued between the Tetrarchs, leading to a return to internal conflict.

Economic and Administrative Reforms

Diocletian also implemented sweeping economic reforms, including the introduction of price controls to combat inflation and efforts to stabilize the currency. He reorganized the military, increasing the number of legions and reinforcing frontier defenses, but these measures came at a high cost, leading to even heavier taxation and further straining the population.

In addition to military reforms, Diocletian restructured the administrative system of the Empire. He increased the number of provinces, making it easier to govern and manage resources. This decentralization, however, also led to more bureaucratic inefficiency and corruption, which became increasingly evident in the later years of the Empire.

Constantine the Great and Christianity

The reign of Constantine the Great (reigned 306–337 AD) represents a crucial moment in the history of the Roman Empire, not only for his military and administrative reforms but also for his role in the establishment of Christianity as a dominant force in the Empire.

Constantine's Rise to Power

Constantine's rise to power was marked by civil war. Following the death of his father, Constantius, Constantine fought rival emperors in a series of battles, culminating in the decisive Battle of the Milvian Bridge in 312 AD. Before this battle, Constantine famously saw a vision of a Christian cross in the sky, accompanied by the words "In this sign, you will conquer." Constantine, already sympathetic to Christianity, took this as a divine sign and adopted the Christian symbol on his soldiers' shields.

Constantine the Great

With his victory at Milvian Bridge, Constantine became the undisputed ruler of the western half of the Roman Empire, and soon after, he became the sole emperor. His reign would be marked by a shift in the Empire's religious landscape.

The Edict of Milan and the Rise of Christianity

In 313 AD, Constantine, alongside Licinius (Emperor of the East), issued the Edict of Milan, which granted religious tolerance to all religions, effectively legalizing Christianity within the Empire. This was a pivotal moment for Christians, who had long been persecuted under previous emperors. Constantine himself was baptized on his deathbed, cementing his legacy as a protector of the Christian faith.

Constantine also moved the capital of the Empire from Rome to Byzantium, renaming it Constantinople. This would eventually become the heart of the Byzantine Empire and the center of Christian power in the East.

Barbarian Invasions and the Sack of Rome (410)

By the end of the 4th century, the Western Roman Empire was severely weakened by a combination of internal instability and external threats. One of the most significant pressures came from the barbarian invasions.

Various groups, such as the Visigoths, Vandals, Franks, and Huns, pushed against Rome's borders. The Huns, led by the fearsome Attila, were perhaps the greatest threat, sweeping through Eastern and Western Europe, forcing many tribes to flee into Roman territory.

In 410 AD, the Visigoths, led by Alaric I, famously sacked Rome. This was the first time in nearly 800 years that Rome had been breached by an enemy, a traumatic event that shocked the Roman world and symbolized the decline of the Western Empire. The fall of Rome did not immediately mean the end of the Empire, but it was a harbinger of the inevitable collapse.

The Fall of the Western Roman Empire (476 AD)

Despite the continued efforts of Roman emperors to restore stability, the Western Roman Empire was in its death throes. The final blow came in 476 AD when the last Roman emperor in the West, Romulus Augustulus, was deposed by the Germanic chieftain Odoacer.

Odoacer, rather than declaring himself emperor, sent the imperial regalia to the Eastern Roman Emperor, Zeno, symbolizing the end of Roman rule in the West. While the Eastern Empire, now known as the Byzantine Empire, continued for another thousand years, the Western Empire ceased to exist, marking the official fall of Rome.

The collapse of the Western Roman Empire was the result of a combination of internal and external factors. Internal decay, political instability, economic collapse, and military decline, weakened the Empire's ability to defend itself against external threats. The barbarian invasions, which had begun decades earlier, had finally overwhelmed the crumbling infrastructure of the Western Roman Empire.

The Legacy of the Fall

The fall of the Western Roman Empire did not mean the end of Roman civilization. The Eastern Roman Empire, with its capital in Constantinople, continued to thrive for another thousand years, preserving Roman culture, law, and traditions. Furthermore, the Roman Catholic Church, which had risen to prominence during the reign of Constantine, became a powerful force in medieval Europe, helping to preserve many aspects of Roman society and thought.

Rome's legacy, from its political systems to its legal innovations, continued to shape the world long after the Empire's fall. The lessons of Rome, its rise, its decline, and its ability to influence later generations, remain relevant to this day, reminding us of the fragility of power and the enduring nature of empire.

In the next chapter, we will turn our attention to the Eastern Roman Empire and its remarkable survival as the Byzantine Empire, examining its achievements and its lasting influence on the medieval world.

CHAPTER 14: THE EASTERN EMPIRE AND BYZANTIUM

The fall of the Western Roman Empire in 476 AD marked the end of a chapter in the history of Rome, but the story was far from over. While the West crumbled under the weight of internal strife and barbarian invasions, the Eastern Roman Empire, later known as the Byzantine Empire, not only survived but thrived for nearly a thousand years. Its capital, Constantinople, became the new heart of Roman power, a symbol of resilience and continuity amidst the collapse of its Western counterpart. This chapter will explore the survival of the Eastern Empire, the glory of Constantinople, the reign of Justinian the Great, and the lasting legacy of the Byzantine Empire in law, culture, and Christianity.

Survival of the Eastern Roman Empire

While the Western Roman Empire crumbled in 476 AD, the Eastern Roman Empire remained intact, maintaining its imperial structure and cultural identity. The division between the Eastern and Western halves of the Roman Empire was not a sudden break but a gradual process that had begun long before the Western Empire's collapse. The East had always been wealthier, more stable, and more defensible than the West, which was plagued by economic difficulties and barbarian invasions.

After the fall of Rome, the Eastern Roman Empire, with its capital at Constantinople (modern-day Istanbul), continued to prosper. The Empire's survival was in part due to its strategic position between Europe and Asia, which allowed it to control crucial trade routes, as well as its highly fortified capital, which was difficult to breach.

Byzantium, as it was often called by later historians, was not a new empire in the strictest sense. It was simply a continuation of the Roman Empire, carrying the traditions, laws, and ideals of Rome into a new era. Despite the loss of the western provinces, the Eastern Empire, under the leadership of emperors in Constantinople, remained a significant power for centuries.

Constantinople as the New Rome

The establishment of Constantinople as the new capital of the Roman Empire in 330 AD by Emperor Constantine the Great was a watershed moment in Roman history. The city, originally known as Byzantium, was strategically located on the Bosporus Strait, offering a perfect position for trade and defense. Constantine, after consolidating power, chose the city for its strategic advantages and its symbolic potential.

Constantinople was designed to be the "New Rome," both in terms of its political and cultural significance. Constantine wanted to create a city that would rival Rome in its grandeur, one that would become a beacon of Christian orthodoxy and imperial power. He adorned the city with monumental buildings, churches, and public works, ensuring it would become the political and religious heart of the Eastern Roman Empire.

The city's location also made it the gateway between Europe and Asia, and it quickly became the epicenter of trade, culture, and diplomacy in the medieval world. Constantinople was fortified with impressive walls, making it one of the most defensible cities in the world. The Walls of Theodosius, built in the 5th century, are a testament to the city's resilience, withstanding numerous sieges over the centuries.

For almost a thousand years, Constantinople served as the center of the Byzantine Empire. It was the seat of the emperor, the center of the Orthodox Christian Church, and the hub of Byzantine culture, art, and learning. Despite the gradual decline of Byzantine power in later centuries, the city remained an enduring symbol of Roman heritage.

Justinian and the Reconquest of Lost Territories

Perhaps the most famous Byzantine emperor was Justinian I, who reigned from 527 to 565 AD. His reign marked a high point in the history of the Byzantine Empire, characterized by territorial expansion, monumental building projects, and significant legal reforms.

Mosaic of Justinian I

The Reconquest of the West

One of Justinian's primary goals was to restore the former glory of the Roman Empire, particularly in the West. Although the Western Roman Empire had fallen in the 5th century, Justinian sought to reconquer the lost territories and restore imperial control over the Mediterranean. His ambitious campaign, known as the Justinianic Reconquest, aimed to reclaim the western provinces that had been lost to the barbarian invasions.

In the 530s, Justinian's general Belisarius led a series of successful military campaigns in North Africa, Italy, and Spain. The first major success came in 533 AD with the defeat of the Vandals in North Africa. After this victory, Belisarius moved into Italy, where the Byzantine forces successfully pushed out the Ostrogoths and reestablished imperial control over the Italian Peninsula. The reconquest also extended to parts of Spain and the Balearic Islands.

Despite these successes, the reconquests were ultimately short-lived. The empire's military resources were stretched thin, and the territories that Justinian regained were difficult to hold due to both external pressures and internal strife. However, Justinian's reconquests had a profound impact on the historical legacy of the Byzantine Empire, as they briefly restored Roman rule in the West and reinforced the idea of a unified Christian empire.

The Building of Hagia Sophia and Other Monuments

Justinian is also remembered for his monumental building projects. His most famous architectural achievement was the construction of Hagia Sophia in Constantinople, an awe-inspiring church that was completed in 537 AD. The church, which served as the cathedral of Constantinople for nearly 1,000 years, was one of the largest and most innovative buildings of its time. Its vast dome was a feat of engineering and became a symbol of Byzantine religious and artistic achievement.

Hagia Sophia

Justinian also commissioned numerous other works, including the Great Palace of Constantinople, the Hippodrome, and the Walls of Constantinople, all of which contributed to the imperial grandeur of the city.

Byzantine Legacy in Law, Culture, and Christianity

While the Byzantine Empire's military and territorial ambitions were often limited, its legacy in law, culture, and religion was far-reaching.

The Code of Justinian

One of Justinian's most enduring contributions was his work on Roman law. In the 530s, he ordered the compilation of Roman legal texts, leading to the creation of the Corpus Juris Civilis (Body of Civil Law), which became the foundation for legal systems in many parts of Europe. The Code of Justinian, as it is often called, consolidated centuries of legal writings and codified the principles of Roman law. It was a cornerstone of Byzantine administration and later influenced the development of modern legal systems in Europe.

The Corpus Juris Civilis became the model for the legal systems of medieval Europe, especially in the Holy Roman Empire, and continues to be influential in many countries to this day. Its concepts of justice, property rights, and contracts are still evident in modern legal practices.

Byzantine Culture and Learning

Byzantine culture was deeply rooted in the Roman tradition, but it also developed a unique identity, especially after the rise of Christianity. The Byzantines made significant contributions to art, literature, and scholarship. Byzantine art, particularly in the form of mosaics, icons, and religious paintings, had a profound influence on the Eastern Orthodox Church and on later Christian art.

Byzantine scholars preserved and copied many classical texts from the Greek and Roman worlds, ensuring that the intellectual legacy of ancient Greece and Rome was passed down to later generations. In the fields of philosophy, mathematics, and medicine, Byzantine scholars continued to build on the knowledge of earlier civilizations.

Christianity and the Orthodox Church

The Byzantine Empire played a central role in the spread of Christianity. Under Constantine, Christianity was legalized and became the official religion of the Empire, but it was during the Byzantine period that Christianity truly became the defining feature of the Empire. The Byzantine Church, also known as the Eastern Orthodox Church, became a powerful institution, with the Patriarch of Constantinople as its spiritual leader.

The schism between the Eastern Orthodox Church and the Western Catholic Church in 1054 AD further solidified the division between the Eastern and Western halves of Christendom. The Byzantine Empire's role as the protector of Orthodox Christianity meant that it served as a cultural and religious bridge between East and West, and its religious influence extended far beyond its borders, reaching into Russia, the Balkans, and beyond.

The End of the Byzantine Empire

While the Byzantine Empire flourished for centuries, it eventually succumbed to external pressures and internal decline. By the 11th century, the Empire was severely weakened, both by foreign invasions and internal fragmentation. The Fourth Crusade (1204 AD) dealt a severe blow, as Crusaders sacked Constantinople, and the Empire never fully recovered. In 1453 AD, Constantinople was finally conquered by the Ottoman Turks, marking the end of the Byzantine Empire.

Despite its fall, the Byzantine Empire left a lasting legacy. Its preservation of Roman law, its unique Christian culture, and its role in maintaining the knowledge of the ancient world shaped the medieval and early modern periods. The legacy of the Byzantine Empire, particularly its influence on Eastern Christianity and the development of European legal systems, continues to be felt today.

In the next chapter, we will examine the enduring legacy of the Roman Empire, from its contributions to law and governance to its cultural and architectural influence, and explore how the idea of Rome continues to captivate the imagination of the modern world.

CHAPTER 15: THE ENDURING LEGACY OF ROME

Rome may have fallen, but it never truly vanished. Its memory, institutions, and cultural DNA were woven into the fabric of Europe and beyond. For over two millennia, Roman ideas have shaped the worlds of law, government, engineering, literature, and imagination — an empire whose true boundaries stretched not only across land, but through time.

Roman Law, Government, and Infrastructure

Perhaps Rome's most lasting legacy lies in its legal and administrative systems. Roman law, especially as codified under Justinian in the 6th century, became the foundation for legal traditions across much of Europe. Ideas like property rights, contracts, legal precedent, and citizen rights deeply influenced medieval and modern law.

Roman government structures including senates, assemblies, and magistracies, inspired political thought throughout the ages. The U.S. Constitution, the French Republic, and other modern democracies owe much to Roman models of civic responsibility, republican governance, and legal order.

Rome's engineering achievements were equally enduring. Roads, aqueducts, bridges, and sewers were marvels of design and utility, many still in use centuries after Rome's fall. Roman concrete, arches, and domes remain iconic in architecture.

Even today, we measure distance in miles (from Roman mille passus), build on grid patterns first used by Roman surveyors, and walk through cities still aligned with Roman foundations.

Latin Language and Literature

Latin, the language of Rome, did not die with the empire, it evolved. French, Spanish, Italian, Portuguese, and Romanian all descend directly from Latin.

Even English, though Germanic, is saturated with Latin vocabulary through law, science, and religion.

Roman literature shaped Western storytelling. Virgil's Aeneid offered a founding myth of Rome with moral and political overtones. Ovid's Metamorphoses, Cicero's oratory, Seneca's philosophy, and Tacitus' histories remained required reading through the Renaissance and beyond.

Latin also remained the language of the Church, of learning, and of diplomacy throughout the Middle Ages. Universities taught in Latin, papal decrees were issued in Latin, and scientific discoveries were recorded in Latin. It was the language of power and knowledge, a legacy of empire.

Rome and the Modern World

Rome became a touchstone for later ages seeking greatness. The Renaissance rediscovered and revered Roman art, architecture, and literature. Petrarch and Machiavelli studied Roman history for lessons on virtue and political power. Michelangelo and Raphael took direct inspiration from Roman ruins.

In the Enlightenment, Rome's rationalism and republican ideals were held up as the height of civilization. Thinkers like Montesquieu and Jefferson looked to Rome when envisioning new forms of government.

In more authoritarian moments, too, Rome loomed large. Napoleon, Hitler, and Mussolini all claimed to inherit its mantle. The idea of Rome, powerful and orderly, could be molded to suit many ideologies.

Its symbols, the eagle, the SPQR (Latin abbreviation for *"Senatus Populusque Romanus"* which translates to *"The Senate and People of Rome"*) standard, and the fasces, have appeared again and again, both in admiration and appropriation.

Coat of arms of Reggio Emilia municipality

Rome in Popular Imagination

From Hollywood epics to best-selling novels, from video games to marble columns on modern buildings, Rome continues to fascinate. Why?

Because Rome was vast, dramatic, and contradictory. It was a civilization of brutal conquest and great beauty, of emperors and slaves, of innovation and oppression. It feels both ancient and oddly familiar.

Films like Ben-Hur, Gladiator, and Spartacus have brought its spectacles to life. Books like I, Claudius and Eagle of the Ninth have imagined its people. Documentaries, museums, and school curricula keep its memory vivid.

Modern cities echo its form. Capitols and courthouses display Roman columns. Our stadiums resemble amphitheatres. Even the calendar, with months like July (for Julius Caesar) and August (for Augustus), is Roman.

Rome may have lost its empire, but it won immortality.

EPILOGUE: THE SHADOW THAT REMAINS

Rome has passed into history, but not into silence.

Its armies no longer march, its emperors no longer rule, and its temples lie in ruins. Yet across the centuries, the Roman Empire endures, not as a living state, but as a memory, a mirror, and a question. It lingers in the languages we speak, the laws we inherit, and the architecture we admire. It flickers in films, in parliaments, in the layout of cities and the ideals of nations.

The story of Rome is one of astonishing scale, a small city rising to command continents, a republic transformed into autocracy, a world held together by roads, legions, and laws. But it is also a deeply human story: of ambition and anxiety, of reformers and tyrants, of citizens and slaves, poets and peasants. Rome was never just an empire, it was a complex, contradictory world filled with people striving to build, to rule, to endure.

We study Rome not to glorify it, but to understand it, and, perhaps, to understand ourselves. Its legacy is not simple. Rome gave the world systems of justice and ideals of citizenship, yet also left scars of conquest and oppression. It created order and beauty, but also war and silence.

What survives of Rome today is not marble or empire, but influence. It lives on in how we imagine power, how we structure governments, how we think about history and identity. In times of crisis, leaders invoke Rome. In times of peace, so do artists. The name itself has become a symbol, of grandeur, of decay, of something once mighty and never quite gone.

Rome reminds us that no power is permanent, but some ideas are. That even the greatest empires fall, and yet still speak.

We walk among its ruins not only to see what was, but to reflect on what remains.

der's story is a powerful reminder that greatness always carries with it a cost, and that no matter how grand the dream, it is always subject to the limits of time, mortality, and human frailty.

APPENDIX

TIMELINE OF THE ROMAN EMPIRE

The Roman Kingdom (c. 753–509 BC)

- c. 753 BC – Traditional date of the founding of Rome by Romulus
- 753–509 BC – Rule of the Seven Kings of Rome:

o Romulus

o Numa Pompilius

o Tullus Hostilius

o Ancus Marcius

o Lucius Tarquinius Priscus

o Servius Tullius

o Lucius Tarquinius Superbus (last king)

The Roman Republic (509–27 BC)

- 509 BC – Overthrow of the monarchy; establishment of the Republic
- 494 BC – First Secession of the Plebs; creation of the Tribune of the Plebs
- 450 BC – Laws of the Twelve Tables codified
- 390 BC – Sack of Rome by the Gauls
- 264–146 BC – The Punic Wars against Carthage

o 264–241 BC – First Punic War (Sicily won)

- 218–201 BC – Second Punic War (Hannibal's invasion; Rome victorious)
- 149–146 BC – Third Punic War (destruction of Carthage)
  - 133 BC – Reforms and death of Tiberius Gracchus begin era of internal turmoil
  - 107–100 BC – Gaius Marius reforms the Roman army
  - 82–79 BC – Dictatorship of Lucius Cornelius Sulla
  - 60 BC – First Triumvirate: Julius Caesar, Pompey, Crassus
  - 49 BC – Caesar crosses the Rubicon; civil war begins
  - 44 BC – Assassination of Julius Caesar
  - 43 BC – Second Triumvirate: Octavian, Antony, Lepidus
  - 31 BC – Battle of Actium: Octavian defeats Antony and Cleopatra

The Roman Empire – Principate (27 BC – 284 AD)

- 27 BC – Octavian becomes Augustus, the first emperor; start of Empire

Julio-Claudian Dynasty:

- Augustus (27 BC – 14 AD)
- Tiberius (14–37 AD)
- Caligula (37–41)
- Claudius (41–54)
- Nero (54–68)

Year of the Four Emperors (69 AD) – Galba, Otho, Vitellius, Vespasian

Flavian Dynasty:

- Vespasian (69–79)
- Titus (79–81) – Eruption of Vesuvius, destruction of Pompeii
- Domitian (81–96)

Nerva-Antonine Dynasty:

- Nerva (96–98)
- Trajan (98–117) – Empire reaches greatest extent
- Hadrian (117–138) – Hadrian's Wall built in Britain
- Antoninus Pius (138–161)
- Marcus Aurelius (161–180) – Stoic philosopher-king
- Commodus (180–192)

Crisis of the Third Century (235–284):

- Frequent turnover of emperors, civil wars, invasions, plague
- Notable emperors: Decius, Valerian, Gallienus, Aurelian

The Roman Empire – Dominate (284–476 in West; to 1453 in East)

- 284 CE – Diocletian becomes emperor; begins Tetrarchy (rule by four)
- 312 – Battle of the Milvian Bridge: Constantine defeats Maxentius
- 313 – Edict of Milan: Constantine legalizes Christianity
- 324 – Constantine reunites empire; founds Constantinople
- 337 – Death of Constantine

- 395 – Death of Theodosius I; permanent split into Western and Eastern Empires

Fall of the Western Roman Empire (476 AD)

- 410 – Sack of Rome by Visigoths under Alaric
- 455 – Sack of Rome by Vandals
- 476 – Deposition of Romulus Augustulus, last Western Roman emperor, by Odoacer. Traditional date for the fall of the Western Roman Empire

The Eastern Roman (Byzantine) Empire (330–1453)

- 527–565 – Reign of Justinian I; reconquers parts of West, codifies Roman law (Corpus Juris Civilis)
- 610–641 – Reign of Heraclius; Greek replaces Latin in administration
- 726–843 – Period of Iconoclasm (conflict over use of religious images)
- 1054 – Great Schism: Split between Roman Catholic and Eastern Orthodox churches
- 1204 – Sack of Constantinople by Crusaders (Fourth Crusade)
- 1261 – Byzantines reclaim Constantinople
- 1453 – Fall of Constantinople to the Ottoman Turks. Marks the final end of the Roman Empire

GLOSSARY OF ROMAN TERMS AND TITLES

People and Social Classes

- Patrician – A member of the Roman aristocracy; the elite class in the early Republic.

- Plebeian – A common citizen of Rome; initially excluded from political power but later gained rights.

- Equestrian (Equites) – A social class between the senators and plebeians, often wealthy and involved in business or administration.

- Freedman (Libertus) – A former slave who had been granted freedom; could become a Roman citizen with limited rights.

- Slave (Servus) – A person legally owned by another; essential to the Roman economy and society.

- Client – A lower-status Roman who depended on a patron for support in exchange for loyalty and services.

- Paterfamilias – The male head of a Roman household; had legal authority over the family.

Political and Legal Terms

- Senate (Senatus) – The central governing body of the Republic and later the Empire, composed mostly of aristocrats.

- Consul – One of two annually elected chief magistrates in the Roman Republic who led the government and army.

- Dictator – A magistrate given absolute power temporarily during a state emergency, usually for six months.

- Tribune of the Plebs (Tribunus Plebis) – An official elected to protect plebeian interests; had veto power.

- Praetor – A judicial magistrate responsible for civil and criminal law, and later provincial governance.

- Censor – An official in charge of conducting the census, overseeing public morality, and supervising public contracts.

- Aedile – An official responsible for city maintenance, public games, and grain supply.

- Quaestor – An entry-level magistrate responsible for financial matters.

- Tetrarchy – The system of rule by four emperors introduced by Diocletian to stabilize the Empire.

- Imperator – Originally a title for victorious generals; later synonymous with emperor.

- Princeps – Meaning "first citizen," the title adopted by Augustus to suggest a republican appearance of rule.

- Augustus – A title meaning "the revered one," granted to Octavian; used by all later emperors.

- Caesar – Originally Julius Caesar's family name, it became a title for emperors and their heirs.

- Leges – Laws passed by the Roman assemblies or decreed by the emperor.

- Pax Romana – The "Roman Peace," a long period of stability and prosperity across the empire (27 BC – 180 AD).

Military Terms

- Legion (Legio) – The basic unit of the Roman army, typically composed of 4,000–6,000 soldiers.

- Centurion – A professional officer in charge of a century (around 80–100 soldiers) within a legion.

- Auxiliaries (Auxilia) – Non-citizen troops who supported the legions; could gain citizenship after service.

- Limes – The fortified frontiers of the Roman Empire, such as Hadrian's Wall or the Danube border.

- Triumph – A ceremonial parade granted to victorious generals by the Senate.

- Cohort – A subdivision of the legion, consisting of 480 soldiers.

- Decurion – A cavalry officer or a local town councillor, depending on context.

Religious and Cultural Terms

- Pontifex Maximus – The chief priest of the Roman state religion; later a title held by emperors.

- Augur – A priest who interpreted the will of the gods by studying the flight of birds.

- Lares and Penates – Household gods worshipped by Roman families.

- Mystery cults – Secretive religious groups such as those of Mithras or Isis, popular in the Empire.

- Imperial cult – The worship of emperors as gods, especially in the provinces.

- Forum – The central public square in Roman cities, used for markets, politics, and social life.

- Villa – A country estate or rural farm, often owned by the wealthy.

- Domus – A Roman house typically occupied by the upper classes in cities.

Infrastructure and Daily Life

- Aqueduct – A structure used to transport water into cities and towns.

- Thermae – Public baths used for hygiene, relaxation, and socializing.

- Via – Latin for "road"; Roman roads like the Via Appia connected the empire.

- Insula – A multi-storey apartment building that housed the urban poor and middle classes.

- Basilica – A public building used for business and legal matters; later adopted by Christian churches.

- Circus – A large open-air venue for chariot racing (e.g., Circus Maximus).

- Amphitheatre – A circular or oval arena used for gladiatorial games and spectacles (e.g., Colosseum).

- Toga – A formal garment worn by Roman male citizens.

LIST OF EMPERORS

The following is a chronological list of Roman Emperors with their dates of rule. For clarity and manageability, this list includes the major emperors from the unified Roman Empire, the Crisis of the Third Century, the division into Eastern and Western empires, and the early Byzantine period.

Julio-Claudian Dynasty (27 BC – 68 AD)

1. Augustus (Octavian) – 27 BC to 14 AD

2. Tiberius – 14 to 37

3. Caligula (Gaius) – 37 to 41

4. Claudius – 41 to 54

5. Nero – 54 to 68

Year of the Four Emperors (69 AD)

6. Galba – 68 to 69

7. Otho – 69

8. Vitellius – 69

9. Vespasian – 69 to 79

Flavian Dynasty (69 – 96)

10. Titus – 79 to 81

11. Domitian – 81 to 96

Nerva–Antonine Dynasty (96 – 192)

12. Nerva – 96 to 98

13. Trajan – 98 to 117

14. Hadrian – 117 to 138

15. Antoninus Pius – 138 to 161

16. Marcus Aurelius – 161 to 180

17. Lucius Verus (co-emperor) – 161 to 169

18. Commodus – 180 to 192

Year of the Five Emperors (193) and Severan Dynasty (193 – 235)

19. Pertinax – 193

20. Didius Julianus – 193

21. Septimius Severus – 193 to 211

22. Caracalla – 198 to 217 (joint with Severus until 211)

23. Geta (co-emperor) – 209 to 211

24. Macrinus – 217 to 218

25. Elagabalus – 218 to 222

26. Severus Alexander – 222 to 235

Crisis of the Third Century (235 – 284)
(A period of rapid turnover, civil wars, and multiple claimants. Not all "emperors" are listed.)

27. Maximinus Thrax – 235 to 238

28. Gordian I and II – 238 (brief reign)

29. Pupienus and Balbinus – 238

30. Gordian III – 238 to 244

31. Philip the Arab – 244 to 249

32. Decius – 249 to 251

33. Trebonianus Gallus – 251 to 253

34. Aemilian – 253

35. Valerian – 253 to 260

36. Gallienus – 253 to 268

37. Claudius Gothicus – 268 to 270

38. Quintillus – 270

39. Aurelian – 270 to 275

40. Tacitus – 275 to 276

41. Probus – 276 to 282

42. Carus – 282 to 283

43. Carinus and Numerian – 283 to 285

Tetrarchy and Reunification (284 – 324)

44. Diocletian – 284 to 305

45. Maximian (co-emperor) – 286 to 305

46. Constantius Chlorus – 305 to 306

47. Galerius – 305 to 311

48. Severus II – 306 to 307

49. Maxentius – 306 to 312

50. Constantine the Great – 306 to 337 (sole ruler from 324)

Constantinian and Valentinian Dynasties (337 – 395)

51. Constantius II – 337 to 361

52. Constans – 337 to 350

53. Constantine II – 337 to 340

54. Julian the Apostate – 361 to 363

55. Jovian – 363 to 364

56. Valentinian I – 364 to 375

57. Valens – 364 to 378 (Eastern Emperor)

58. Gratian – 367 to 383

59. Valentinian II – 375 to 392

60. Theodosius I – 379 to 395 (last to rule both East and West)

Western Roman Empire (395 – 476)

61. Honorius – 395 to 423

62. Valentinian III – 425 to 455

63. Petronius Maximus – 455

64. Avitus – 455 to 456

65. Majorian – 457 to 461

66. Libius Severus – 461 to 465

67. Anthemius – 467 to 472

68. Olybrius – 472

69. Glycerius – 473 to 474

70. Julius Nepos – 474 to 475

71. Romulus Augustulus – 475 to 476 (deposed by Odoacer — traditional end of the Western Roman Empire)

Eastern Roman (Byzantine) Emperors (selected early rulers)

72. Arcadius – 395 to 408

73. Theodosius II – 408 to 450

74. Marcian – 450 to 457

75. Leo I – 457 to 474

76. Zeno – 474 to 491

77. Anastasius I – 491 to 518

78. Justin I – 518 to 527

79. Justinian I – 527 to 565 (reconquered much of the West, codified Roman law)

ABOUT THE AUTHOR

I am a passionate military and history writer whose love for the past was kindled by family stories. One grandfather endured four years as a prisoner of war in Poland during World War 2, while my great-grandfather fought at the Somme in World War 1 — a legacy that ignited a lifelong fascination with courage, conflict, and the human spirit in wartime.

In 2024, after receiving a diagnosis of stage 4 cancer, I turned to writing with newfound purpose. The act of storytelling has become a welcome distraction for me! As of July 2025, I've completed 34 cycles of fortnightly chemotherapy, a treatment that continues — but so does my writing, undeterred and determined.

Whether I'm exploring the battles of World War II, the legends of Greek mythology, the intrigue of Roman emperors, or the ambition of Alexander the Great, I write to inspire curiosity in readers, both young and old, and make history come alive with meaning.

I live in the Cotswolds with my wife, my two children, and two lovely black Labradors. When not writing or reading, you'll likely find me wandering the hills dreaming up my next journey into the past.

See more at: ***james-burrows.com* and *@burrowsauthor***.

If you'd like to read more, you can find all my books at:

USA Readers

UK Readers

www.ingramcontent.com/pod-product-compliance
Lightning Source LLC
Chambersburg PA
CBHW071207070526
44584CB00019B/2942